BABY STORYTIME MAGIC

ALA Editions purchases fund advocacy,
awareness, and accreditation programs
for library professionals worldwide.

BABY STORYTIME MAGIC

Active Early Literacy through Bounces, Rhymes, Tickles, and More

Kathy MacMillan and

Christine Kirker

with illustrations by Melanie Fitz

AMERICAN LIBRARY ASSOCIATION

Chicago 2014

KATHY MACMILLAN is a freelance writer, American Sign Language interpreter, and storyteller. She is the author of *Try Your Hand at This! Easy Ways to Incorporate Sign Language into Your Programs* (Scarecrow Press, 2006), *A Box Full of Tales* (ALA Editions, 2008), and *Little Hands and Big Hands: Children and Adults Signing Together* (Huron Street Press, 2013), and coauthor of *Storytime Magic* (ALA Editions, 2009), *Kindergarten Magic* (ALA Editions, 2011), and *Multicultural Storytime Magic* (ALA Editions, 2012). She was the library/media specialist at the Maryland School for the Deaf from 2001 to 2005 and prior to that was a children's librarian at Carroll County (Maryland) Public Library and Howard County (Maryland) Library, where she developed and presented hundreds of programs for all ages. She holds a master of library science degree from the University of Maryland, College Park, and has been reviewing for *School Library Journal* since 1999. She presents American Sign Language programs and resources through www.storiesbyhand.com and offers storytime resources at www.storytimestuff.net.

CHRISTINE KIRKER is a library associate with the Carroll County (Maryland) Public Library. Since joining the library staff in 2005, Christine has developed and presented many programs for children of all ages, including monthly preschool science programs. She is the coauthor of *Storytime Magic* (ALA Editions, 2009), *Kindergarten Magic* (ALA Editions, 2011), and *Multicultural Storytime Magic* (ALA Editions, 2012). Previously, Christine spent ten years at the University of Maryland, Baltimore County (UMBC) as a research analyst for the Office of Institutional Research. She graduated from UMBC in 1992. Christine presents trainings and programs introducing ways to enhance storytimes through www.storytimestuff.net.

The American Sign Language (ASL) graphic images in this book can be found in *American Sign Language Clip and Create 5,* a software product of the Institute for Disabilities Research and Training (IDRT), and are used here with the permission of the publisher. To purchase a copy or learn more about IDRT's other ASL-accessible software, visit www.idrt.com.

Printed in the United States of America

18 17 16 15 14   5 4 3 2 1

While extensive effort has gone into ensuring the reliability of the information in this book, the publisher makes no warranty, express or implied, with respect to the material contained herein. We have made every effort to provide accurate pronunciation guides for the foreign language materials in this book; we acknowledge, however, that pronunciations by native users may vary due to the dynamic nature of language across settings and regions.

ISBN: 978-0-8389-1216-4 (paper).

Library of Congress Control Number: 2013049729

Cover design by Kirstin Krutsch. Images © Shutterstock, Inc.
Book design by Karen Sheets de Gracia in Candy Randy, Kristen ITC, Georgia, and Helvetica.
Composition by Dianne M. Rooney.

♾ This paper meets the requirements of ANSI/NISO Z39.48–1992 (Permanence of Paper).

For JX, who will always be my baby corn.

—KM

For my babies, Ashleigh and Sean, who are almost all grown up, and Ava, Maya, and Henry, who have years to go.

—CMK

Contents

WEB **Flannelboard patterns, craft patterns, and worksheets are available online at alaeditions.org/webextras.**

Acknowledgments

THANK YOU TO the people who made this project possible:

- The fantastic team at ALA Editions who put it all together!
- Brandt Ensor for contributing "Bathtime Fun."
- Melanie Fitz for her beautiful illustrations.
- Louise Rollins for her insightful comments on the theory and practice of early childhood education.
- The many workshop participants and newsletter contributors who have inspired us with their enthusiasm and ideas!

Developing Brains, Developing Literacy

WHETHER YOU'VE BEEN presenting baby storytimes for fifteen years or fifteen minutes, you probably already know that the first five years of life are key for brain development and early literacy. Many public libraries have instituted baby and toddler programs, but finding exciting materials for baby storytime that go beyond Mother Goose can be a challenge. Enter *Baby Storytime Magic*—a treasure trove of new and exciting ideas for baby programs featuring age-appropriate book recommendations, fingerplays, bounces, flannelboards, American Sign Language activities, and more, all of which revolve around themes from a baby's world. Throughout the chapters that follow, you will find these items arranged by type of material, with a thematic index to provide maximum access. Each entry is accompanied by a *literacy bit,* a suggested script for explaining to caregivers the benefits of the activity and how to use it at home. Visit www.alaeditions.org/webextras to download full-sized patterns for all flannelboards and stick puppets.

Involving Caregivers in Baby Storytimes

Baby storytimes differ from storytimes for other age groups because the target audience is not the child, but the caregiver. After all, some of the tiny creatures who enter our storytime rooms cannot see farther than a foot or so—just far enough to see the loving grown-ups who tend to their needs. Learning in early childhood happens in the context of relationships, and so it is our job to foster those relationships in our programs, providing caregivers with tools and techniques to develop language and literacy in their charges. As Sue McLeaf Nespeca (1994) puts it, "The baby attends so the adult can practice!"

And many adults need the practice, because the interactions that build a foundation for literacy do not always come naturally. Caregivers may not know how to interact over a picture book or share a fingerplay with a baby, or may not realize why those interactions are important building blocks to language and not simply distractions to keep baby busy. The most effective baby storytime presenters share early literacy information in an engaging way *and* model fingerplays, songs, and books to use with babies so that caregivers can pick up and extend these techniques in everyday interactions. That is why we have included the literacy bits with each entry in this book. Each bit is designed to be shared before or after the entry it is paired with, in order to give adults concrete examples of early literacy information in action.

In your programs, encourage adult-child interaction by inviting caregivers to sit on the floor or on a chair with the children. Build in interactions through tickle rhymes, choral reading, or fingerplays. Sometimes you may need to direct this interaction explicitly—for example, by asking caregivers to pull children onto their laps as you begin lap bounces.

Be careful, however, not to lecture caregivers about what they should or shouldn't be doing. Parents in particular are under enough pressure in our society, after all, and if they made it to a storytime, they've already shown that they value early literacy enough to attend! Provide resources, modeling, and enthusiasm for literacy development—but not judgments.

Baby's Developing Brain

Because the brain is still developing in the first five years of life, this period is vital for a child's cognitive, emotional, and social development. The pathways between the brain's nerve cells, called synapses, develop during this time. *One thousand trillion* synapses form in the first eight months alone! A child's experiences during this time have a huge impact; the synapses that receive the most stimulation become stronger, while those with little or no stimulation are pruned away. The brain adapts to the input it receives, and around twelve months of age, the pruning process speeds up, deleting connections that have not received repeated stimulation. This means that by providing young children with engaging, quality language and communication experiences in the first year, we lay the foundation for later learning and literacy.

Many wonderful books focus extensively on the stages of early childhood development; see appendix A for recommended titles. Here we offer a condensed list of developmental milestones to give storytime programmers a broad overview of basic child development. Children may vary widely depending on their environment, family history, and special needs. Individual children may also develop at different rates in different areas.

The following paragraphs synthesize information from several sources: Maddigan and Drennan (2003), Marino and Houlihan (1992), Mayes and Cohen (2002), Nespeca (1994), Shelov and Altmann (2009), and Shonkoff and Phillips (2000).

Birth to Three Months

Babies at this age are just beginning to discover the world. They can see faces in their immediate line of vision, but no farther away. In fact, babies are attracted to faces, and their most important task at this age is to develop a trusting relationship with the primary caregiver. Babies are drawn to the sound of the human voice and will generally go quiet at the sound of a familiar one. They will coo and gurgle, but do not yet understand that sounds have meaning. By the end of this period, babies typically can hold up their heads and enjoy playing with their hands and fingers. They will also copy simple movements and facial expressions, laying the foundation for communication and social awareness. At this stage, the brain is forming mental connections quickly and is organized to take in all sounds.

Three to Six Months

Babies begin to interact with the world more by turning toward sounds, smiling, laughing, crying to express emotion, and babbling with single sounds, such as "buh" or "mah." They begin to develop hand-eye coordination (for example, by seeing a toy and then reaching for it). They can now see and track things in their environment and can lift their heads unsupported. They recognize familiar people by sight and like looking in mirrors and looking at faces. By the end of this stage, most babies can pass objects from one hand to the other and can roll from front to back or back to front.

Six to Nine Months

Babies begin to string sounds together in their babbling (for example, "mamamama" instead of just "mah") and become interested in copying sounds and gestures made by others. In this stage, babies start to become aware that something exists even if it is hidden, leading to interest in games like peekaboo. At just eight months of age, babies begin to understand words or signs out of their usual context. By this time, most babies can also sit up independently, recognize familiar faces and sounds, and touch, shake, or drop objects. Most babies will begin to crawl during this time and will pull themselves up to a standing position around the end of this period.

Nine to Twelve Months

At this age, babies may interact with others more—putting out an arm or leg to help with dressing, making sounds to get attention, or even speaking simple words. A baby's individual personality begins to show, and he or she may show preference for certain toys, books, or people. At this age, babies can respond to simple requests. Their babbling begins to sound more like spoken language, even if the words are still incomprehensible. They continue to explore things in their environment in new ways, perhaps by throwing or banging. Most babies take their first steps and say their first word or two during this time.

Twelve to Eighteen Months

At this age, babies interact with others even more and often become curious about other children. They like to hand things to other people, show affection, and point, sign, or talk. At this age, children may begin to explore their environment alone but generally still like to have a caregiver close by. By the age of eighteen months, most children can say several individual words and use them to communicate basic needs and wants and can also follow simple, one-step commands such as "Give me the book."

Eighteen Months to Two Years

Children develop more independence and become very interested in other children. They do not quite know how to play with other children yet, so they may play beside them instead. They love to copy older children and adults. At this age, children may assert their growing sense of independence by becoming defiant. By age two, most children can say simple two- to four-word sentences, follow two-part directions, and point to objects or pictures when named. They begin to sort shapes and colors and may engage in pretend play. They may also begin to use one hand more than the other. Physically, children at this age develop very quickly, learning how to kick a ball, run, climb, walk up and down stairs, and stand on tiptoe.

Key Early Literacy Skills

When it comes to early literacy, the most important point to understand (and to emphasize to the caregivers in your programs) is this: *early literacy* does not mean *early reading*! Perhaps a more accurate term would be *pre-literacy*. *Early literacy* refers to the skills developed in early interactions with caregivers that lay the foundation for language and literacy. Multiple studies show that children who receive direct teaching of reading and writing before they are developmentally ready for it experience higher levels of attention deficit/hyperactivity disorder (ADHD), dyslexia, and other learning disabilities (Johnson 2007). In contrast, children who are exposed to a healthy variety of experiences with language and books are more likely to develop key skills that will help them with literacy, communication, and school readiness.

As adults, we often take for granted the many small skills and bits of knowledge that make up successful reading: the facts that books have covers and contain pictures and text, that books must be held right side up for reading, that print runs from left to right and top to bottom (at least in Western culture!), and that written and spoken language are different from each other (Odean 2003). By illuminating these building blocks for caregivers, we give them the tools to introduce and reinforce early literacy concepts in their interactions with the children in their care.

The National Institute of Child Health and Human Development identifies six key early literacy skills:

1. *Print motivation* refers to a child's interest in printed materials of all kinds: books, signs, labels, name tags, magazines, and so forth. As children develop the understanding that words provide information, stories, and communication, they become more motivated to learn to read and understand the messages the words convey.

2. *Phonological awareness* is the ability to hear and manipulate smaller sounds within words. When babies babble in single or multiple syllables, they are experimenting with the sounds they hear others making. These sounds are the building blocks of speech. Phonological awareness also involves learning to hear how words are similar to and different from one another (for example, by understanding that two words rhyme because their end sounds are the same).

3. *Vocabulary* means knowing and understanding (and eventually using) words. The more children interact with caring adults, the more their vocabularies will develop. The best vocabulary development happens in context—for example, when a caregiver describes what a child is experiencing. A caregiver who says, "Look, the doggie is panting! His tongue is hanging out of his mouth and he is breathing heavily," gives his or her child a rich language experience by labeling what the child is seeing and introducing new words in a concrete context, which builds stronger brain connections than introducing words in isolation. Reading books is a vital way to develop vocabulary because books generally contain more varied and specific vocabulary than caregivers and children use in their day-to-day lives.

4. *Narrative skills* concern the ability to describe things and tell stories. Through listening to books and stories, children internalize sequencing, story structure, and the idea that a story has a beginning, a middle, and an end.

5. *Print awareness* encompasses the nitty-gritty skills of reading, such as noticing print, knowing how to hold a book and turn pages, and knowing how to follow words on a page. Again, babies begin to internalize these skills with repeated exposure to reading stories with caregivers.

6. *Letter knowledge* means knowing the letters of the alphabet and the sounds they make in spoken English. Though fluent readers often forget it, there is no natural connection between the written letters and their corresponding sounds in English or any other language; there is no logical reason why the letter *b* represents the sound at the beginning of the word *bake*—except that it does. This means that learning the letters and the sounds that go with them must happen through exposure and repetition (Ghoting and Martin-Diaz 2005).

Putting It All Together

When you as a programmer have a basic understanding of developmental stages, you can use that information not only to select and present the best materials in your baby storytimes but also to help caregivers understand their children's development and how best to foster it. When you make explicit connections between rhymes and books and the early literacy skills they support, you give caregivers the tools to enhance babies' development every day, not just on library day!

2

Presenting
Baby Storytime

• •

UNDERSTANDING EARLY CHILDHOOD development and the best materials for babies is a necessary foundation for baby storytimes, but there are plenty of logistical issues that can stump even the most creative presenter. In this chapter, we explore some of the practical issues that can determine the success or failure of baby programs.

Age Groupings

As we saw in the child development section in chapter 1, the abilities of a three-month-old differ greatly from those of a twenty-four-month-old. For this reason, many experts recommend offering separate programs for ages birth to twelve months and thirteen to twenty-four months. Author Linda Ernst (2008) recommends doing away with age groupings altogether and focusing instead on developmental stages, offering separate programs for "babes in arms," "wigglers," and "walkers."

Each approach has pros and cons. Because individual babies develop different skills at wildly different rates, organizing your program around a specific age range can mean that you will be working with children at vastly different places in their physical and cognitive development. On the other hand, advertising programs for specific developmental stages can create a barrier, as caregivers may have difficulty figuring out which program is best for their children, or they may have children who are the same age but at different developmental stages.

A larger logistical issue is the practical sustainability of programs geared to too narrow an audience. Even if you have a large population of families with young children, the practicalities of scheduling and staffing may mean that you are able to serve more families by offering two baby programs with broader age ranges instead of one program for babes in arms and another for walkers, or one for ages birth to twelve months and one for ages thirteen to twenty-four months. If your library has a smaller population of families with babies, then setting your age ranges for programs too narrowly is a sure way to decrease attendance.

For this reason, many libraries have settled on a compromise of birth to twenty-four months, or even birth to thirty-six months, as the age range for their baby programs. This approach, too, has pros and cons; while it generally makes for better attendance and staffing for baby programs, it presents challenges to the presenter, who has to match materials to families with babies in various stages of development. In this book, we focus on storytime materials for ages birth to twenty-four months and offer suggestions for adapting activities to babies at different stages. To find ideas for children in the twenty-four- to thirty-six-month age range, see our books *Storytime Magic* (ALA Editions, 2009), *Multicultural Storytime Magic* (ALA Editions, 2012), and *A Box Full of Tales* (ALA Editions, 2007), which feature storytime ideas for ages two and up, with materials especially appropriate for toddlers starred.

The main reason that these mixed-age-group programs work, of course, is that the real audience is not the babies at all, but the caregivers. Another benefit of wider age ranges for baby programs is that it allows families to stay in one group for a longer period, become comfortable with a storytime, and hopefully develop library habits that will continue as their children grow older.

Scheduling

When it comes to scheduling baby storytimes, you must consider your population. Do you have a large percentage of stay-at-home parents? Homeschoolers? In-home day-care providers? If so, weekday programs are a must. But don't forget the working parents, who often look for evening and weekend programs. Also consider siblings' school schedules: Does your baby storytime begin late enough for parents to drop off older children and get to the library? Does baby storytime end early enough for them to pick up siblings from half-day preschool programs? Though it's impossible to adapt your storytime schedule to fit everyone's needs, a bit of research into the major forces shaping the lives of families in your community can save a lot of headaches.

Babies are generally most alert (and least prone to meltdowns) in the morning, so that is generally the best time to schedule baby programs. However, evening programs can be successful if they are held early enough (generally at six or six thirty p.m.) to avoid bedtime conflicts.

The best way to find out the best time for programming in your community is to ask your patrons what they want—and if you want to draw in people who do not already attend storytimes, make sure you go outside your library to survey people! The results may surprise you.

Baby Storytime Format

Babies, of course, generally have short attention spans, so you should not expect the formal part of your storytime to last longer than twenty to thirty minutes. Again, the real audience for these programs is the adults, so providing a space for caregivers to network, share, and ask questions is vital. Many librarians see this informal period (usually conducted as free-play time for the babies while the grown-ups chat) as a less important part of the program, but in fact many caregivers may get more from this unstructured time than they do from the formal program. It is a chance for them to connect, commiserate, share resources, and unwind while their children play nearby in a safe environment. The programmer, however, should not be idle during this time; this is a chance to connect with individual families, suggest resources, and model the early literacy techniques discussed in storytime while interacting with individual children.

Registered or Drop-in?

In all public programs, there is a constant tension between requiring attendees to register for programs and allowing them to drop in. Traditionally, library programs required advance registration; this method allowed programmers to know exactly how many craft items or props were needed, ensured that the group wouldn't be too large for the space, allowed programmers to set group size limits based on what was appropriate for each age group, and made attendees feel "committed" to attending.

In the past fifteen years, however, many libraries have moved to a drop-in model of programming. This shift has often happened because registration requirements have been perceived as a barrier to program attendance, especially for nontraditional library users. Indeed, as families juggle more time commitments and more families have both parents working outside the home, it becomes more difficult for families to commit to programs in advance, particularly for series that run several weeks.

For many libraries, baby programs are the last holdouts that require registration even when all other programs are conducted as drop-ins. The main reason for retaining registration is to keep the group size small. Some libraries, however, have come up with clever and creative solutions that combine the best of both worlds:

> *First come, first served.* A limited number of tickets are available at the information desk beginning thirty minutes before the program.

> *Staggered storytimes.* If space and staffing permit, a second program is offered twenty minutes after the first in another location in the library. This approach could be combined with the ticket approach, with color-coded tickets indicating which program to attend.

Expanded program schedule. Examine your program schedule to fit in more programs. Though it means a quick turnover for the programmer, most libraries can fit three baby and/or toddler programs into the morning hours.

Let it grow. Though it makes the programmer's job easier to have ten babies instead of twenty, it is possible to offer a successful baby storytime with a large group. It takes considerable flexibility on the part of the presenter, and it's important to remember that the program is essentially geared to the adults, not the babies. With a larger storytime, it's even more vital to create interactive experiences for caregiver and child through bounces, choral reading, and shared prop activities. Strategic group management through music is also key; if the babies are growing too loud, getting the adults to join in singing "Twinkle, Twinkle, Little Star" will calm the group down for the next activity. The presenter must also be willing to address ongoing disruptions in a friendly but firm manner.

Siblings in Storytime

When we set out to do our background research for this book, we were shocked at the overwhelmingly negative attitude we found in existing resource books concerning older siblings in baby storytimes. Even those authors who acknowledged the realities of working families and child-care issues seemed to feel that siblings were, at best, a necessary evil to contend with. For example, authors Beth Maddigan and Stefanie Drennan (2003) state that "[t]he presence of children outside the developmental guidelines can be disruptive and cause the children the program was designed for to be uncomfortable."

We take a different view; it is our job as librarians to promote literacy for families, and just as the baby does not exist in a vacuum, neither does his language and literacy development. Older siblings are as much a part of the baby's world as the caregiver; rather than being shunned and dismissed, they should be included and engaged in programs—though never at the expense of the intended audience, of course. Older siblings act as role models for their younger brothers and sisters, and, as objects of fascination for the other babies, can become role models for them too. Families should never be made to feel unwelcome at storytimes. Approval can be conveyed through attitude, but also through making the welcome outright. (For example, for the past eight years, Kathy's "Little Hands Signing" storytimes have included the phrase "Siblings welcome" as part of the program description.)

And yes, it can make the programmer's job a bit more difficult when an older sibling is in attendance, but it's still the programmer's job! As Louise Rollins, early childhood educator at the Maryland School for the Deaf, put it in an e-mail to the authors,

It's important to view the child as part of a family, and work with the whole family . . . It's my job to deal with that—help the kid wait or hold back so the little sibling can participate, and also help the parent see how we modify whatever we're doing to bring it up for an older kid, ask more sophisticated questions of older kids, and so on.

By shifting our perspective and seeing siblings as allies in developing babies' language skills instead of distractions from the "storytime show," we support the baby by supporting the entire family.

Physical Setup

Ideally, baby storytime should happen in a separate space, such as a meeting room. This arrangement not only minimizes distractions for program participants but also allows you to play music, pass out instruments, and allow babies to be babies without disturbing other library patrons. If a separate space is not possible, you can still create a special storytime space within your children's area, or even within open areas in the library, through strategic movement of furniture, bulletin boards, or screens. (In fact, holding your programs "on the floor" once in a while is a great way to advertise—people who might not normally find out about storytimes are more likely to see them!)

The following are some points to consider about the physical setup of your storytime:

Babies spend a lot of time on the floor, so make sure your storytime area is carpeted. If it is not, use a large area rug or foam mat, or ask participants to bring a towel, blanket, or yoga mat to sit on.

If possible, arrange the room so that participants sit in a circle. This placement allows for a feeling of fellowship and emphasizes the idea that storytime is about group participation rather than "entertainment" in which the audience just watches a performer.

Encourage participants to sit on the floor with their babies, but have a few chairs available for those who cannot do so. As the presenter, you may need to sit on a chair or low stool so that everyone can see you. Avoid rocking chairs, which can crush little fingers.

Make sure that your room is baby-safe. The best way to do this is to get down on your hands and knees and look at the room from the baby's point of view, just as new parents are advised to do when babyproofing their houses. Put safety plugs in outlets and make sure that no cords are dangling where babies can get them. If there is a tempting object near floor level, such as a vent, place something in front of it during storytime.

Make sure the floor is clean. You don't want babies finding beads from yesterday's elementary craft program!

Keep your storytime materials hidden in a bag or box, or put them up on a table out of reach. If you have wanderers in your program, ask caregivers at the beginning to please keep babies from touching items on the table or in the bag.

Have everything you need for the program laid out (out of reach) so you don't have to scramble.

If you haven't memorized your rhymes, songs, and so forth, find a place to post the words so that you can look at them quickly without keeping your eyes glued to the page. For baby storytimes, where caregivers also need to know the words, you can post them right on the wall so that everyone can follow along. Flipchart paper is one option, or you can make large printouts of the rhymes and songs that can be seen when posted on the walls. If you do this each time you prepare a storytime, you will develop a library of favorites to draw from. Laminate them or keep them in paper protectors in a binder for easy access.

Place yourself in the least distracting area of the room, away from windows and doors. If possible, position the group so that the entrance is behind them, to minimize distractions from latecomers.

Don't forget the book display! Though it's often overlooked, a book display is an important way to connect concepts in your storytime with materials in your library. Include circulating materials in your display that relate to the program theme or the literacy concepts discussed, and, of course, offer extra copies of any books you read in the program. Even more important, take a few minutes at the end of the program to direct participants' attention to the display and encourage them to check out the materials. Make explicit links between the program content and the materials on the display.

Feedback

When you are in the business of public service, as libraries are, the value of customer feedback cannot be overstated. Whether you are just establishing baby storytimes or have been offering them for some time, build evaluation into your programming process. This may mean asking every caregiver to fill out a brief survey after the program, or handing out cards with a link to an online survey. Keep surveys brief and specific, focusing on the areas you most need to know about. You can use surveys to find out how customers feel about program times, program content, group size, or location and environment. Even if you think you already know the answers, having data in the form of customer survey responses gives you solid evidence and allows you to make a case to your administrators, whether you want to make changes or keep the status quo.

To Theme or Not to Theme

Like the issue of siblings, the issue of whether or not to center your baby storytime around a theme polarizes programmers. Some programmers insist that choosing materials around a theme makes for a smoother storytime experience, while others feel that using themes in baby storytimes leads to the inclusion of material that is not age appropriate.

We advocate a happy medium. Age-appropriateness must be the first consideration when selecting materials for baby storytimes, but that doesn't mean you should pair a rhyme about trains with one about fruit with no apparent transition. Luckily, we live in a time when wonderful books, songs, rhymes, and activities for baby storytimes abound, so it's easier than ever to develop programs around baby-friendly topics that are full of age-appropriate materials. Here is a good rule of thumb: if you can't find enough solid, age-appropriate materials about your desired theme, then that theme is probably not the best fit for baby storytime. It may work better for toddlers or preschoolers, or perhaps if you broaden or tweak your theme a bit, it will fit a baby's world better. For example, "owls" might be too specific as a topic, but "birds" might do just fine. And if you do love themed storytimes, remember that it's okay to throw in something that is not theme related, just because your group loves it (or because you do!).

If you prefer not to use themes in your baby storytimes, you can make your program cohesive through the use of transitional comments and grouping of like elements. A transitional comment can be as simple as this: "That was one of my favorite songs! And here is one of my favorite books to read with babies." You can also transition by grouping materials that support similar early literacy components—such as rhyme, visual tracking, or text-to-self connection—and commenting on these qualities as you move from one item to the next. Comments such as these unify your program elements, whether they are thematically related or not, and give caregivers and children a more fluid experience.

In this book, we have chosen to focus each chapter on one type of storytime material, such as books, bounces, or songs and rhymes. The subject index allows you to find all the entries relating to specific themes. So whether you are a theme lover or not, we've got you covered!

Group Management

For many baby storytime presenters, group management is the most difficult part of the whole endeavor. If you dislike confrontation, then you may worry about how you will handle it when adults chitchat in the background during your stories, let their children pull items off your table, or sit by while a baby screams on and on, disrupting the program.

The best way to prevent these problems is to communicate clear expectations to storytime attendees up front. This may mean posting the guidelines in your children's area or storytime room, communicating them during the registration process (if applicable), or announcing them at the beginning of the program. Keep expectations simple and reasonable, such as these:

> Please turn off your cell phones.

> We understand that children at this age sometimes like to wander, and that's fine, but please keep your child from pulling materials off the table and flannelboard.

> If your child becomes overstimulated and needs a break, please take him out for a few minutes and come back when he's settled down.

> This program is for you as much as your child! Your child will get the most out of it if you participate with her.

If you introduce such expectations at the beginning, then you will be on more solid footing when you reference them later should these issues arise.

Every baby storytime presenter has experienced the child who wanders unchecked in storytime and the caregiver who, for whatever reason, is reluctant to prevent it. In these situations, a firm but playful tone, directed at the child, can do wonders: "Oh, no no no no no! We're not touching the flannelboard right now. Here, let's go visit Mommy . . ."

Another chronic issue in baby storytime is latecomers. Unfortunately, this is part of the landscape of life with young children—just as you get out the door, someone has a poopy diaper or spits up or has to go back and get a lovey. (Honestly, it's a wonder that parents of young children ever make it to storytime at all!) Creating a welcoming environment in storytime means that, rather than chiding latecomers, the presenter needs to find ways to integrate them into the program as quickly as possible. If you have a group that constantly arrives a few minutes late, consider making the first five minutes of your program an informal welcome time, perhaps by taking around a signature puppet or stuffed animal to greet each child. This technique allows everyone to settle in and latecomers to slide in as well.

Your Storytime, Your Style

Ultimately, each programmer will bring his or her own unique style to baby storytime. What works for a bubbly performer type won't work for someone who prefers a quieter, more soothing storytime style. And that's a good thing! Select the materials that get *you* excited about sharing literacy with babies and caregivers, and your excitement will come across to participants, whatever your style. The best storytime presenters have a variety of materials and fallbacks at their fingertips and are ready to switch gears mid-program to match the tenor of the group. Got a fussy group today? Engage the caregivers in some soothing sing-alongs instead of that longer storybook. More babes in arms than you expected? Throw in some extra bouncing rhymes. Don't be afraid to experiment—the worst thing that can happen is that babies get fussy and you move on to something else. (And hey, that can happen even when the material is wildly successful!) It all comes down to attitude—if you genuinely care about welcoming families to the library and sharing early literacy with babies and helping caregivers do the same, your enthusiasm will come across to participants.

3

Books and Book Activities

. . . .

WHEN SELECTING BOOKS for baby storytimes, remember that the focus must be on fostering interaction between caregiver and child. Brief stories with large pictures can work well as group read-alouds, especially if the content of the story invites caregivers to tickle, bounce, or move babies. Smaller books can work well if you have enough copies for each caregiver to hold one. (See the "Choral Reading" section on page 31 for more information about this technique.) Unlike storytimes for other age groups, however, book reading should not make up the bulk of your storytime—a baby storytime may contain only one or two books, or even no books at all! The purpose of reading a book in a baby storytime is quite different from the purpose of reading one in a storytime for older children—here the focus must be on modeling reading techniques that foster early literacy skills so that caregivers can replicate them at home.

1 **Adler, Victoria. *All of Baby Nose to Toes*. New York: Dial, 2009.**

Baby's family members celebrate her from head to toe. Invite caregivers to tickle their babies' eyes, ears, nose, tummy, legs, and toes as they are mentioned in the text. Follow up with the classic song "Head, Shoulders, Knees, and Toes," Baby Hugs (p. 34), or Sticker on My Knee (p. 41).

Literacy bit: "Babies are very interested in their own bodies, as they are learning that they are different from other people. Books and activities that label parts of the body help babies develop vocabulary and self-awareness."

2 **Adler, Victoria.** *Baby, Come Away.* **New York: Farrar, Strauss and Giroux, 2011.**

A bird, a cat, a dog, and a fish each invite a baby to come spend a perfect day resting in a nest, playing with yarn, playing catch, and swimming in the sea, but Baby knows that the best part is coming home to Mommy at day's end.

Consider using this book, along with animal puppets, to organize your program. Introduce a puppet and then read that animal's section of the book. Pause your reading to share songs and rhymes relating to that animal. End with the section in which the baby returns to Mommy's arms, and share a snuggly closing song.

Literacy bit: "Play is the job of young children. The baby in this story explores the natural world and exercises muscles and imagination through play. Play is how young children apply concepts they have learned, experiment, and make sense of their world. Child's play is actually hard work!"

3 **Aylesworth, Jim.** *Cock-a-doodle-doo, Creak, Pop-pop, Moo.* **New York: Holiday House, 2012.**

Follow along to the rhythm and rhyme of the text as a family goes through their day on a farm. For greater emphasis, ask caregivers to repeat the rhythmic text as you read it.

Literacy bit: "Rhyming stories, especially those with strong rhythm, draw attention to the sounds of language. Rhythmic stories and songs help young children hear how words are broken up into syllables more clearly than everyday speech."

4 **Beaumont, Karen.** *Baby Danced the Polka.* **New York: Dial, 2004.**

Baby doesn't want to stay in bed, but prefers to boogie-woogie with the goat, cha-cha with the cow, and shooby-dooby with the sheep. The bouncy rhythm and repetition in this text are perfect for baby storytimes. For maximum impact, use a slow, rhythmic voice when reading the parts where Mama and Daddy put the baby to bed while caregivers rock their children in their laps, and then read the dancing parts in a boisterous voice while the caregivers and babies dance!

Literacy bit: "Whenever you give your child an experience of opposites, such as loud and soft, fast and slow, or high and low, you are helping those brain connections form!"

5 **Bell, Babs.** *The Bridge Is Up!* **New York: HarperCollins, 2004.**

This bright book tells the tale of a drawbridge that is up. A series of vehicles come to cross, but they all have to wait. Finally, when the bridge goes down, they cross. The plot is simple, but the bouncy language and cumulative structure make for a pleasing read-aloud.

After you read the book, give each child a picture of a vehicle and invite caregivers and children to help you act out the story. Create a drawbridge by placing a foam mat upright in your storytime room. Line up the children and caregivers holding their pictures, and tell the story following the pattern in the book. Finally, lay the foam mat flat and let everyone pass over it, cheering.

Literacy bit: "Sequencing activities like this one encourage turn-taking and patience, which are vital skills for effective communication. Even if your child doesn't know how to be patient and take turns just yet, when you participate in activities like these, you are conveying their value."

6 Brown, Margaret Wise. *A Child's Good Morning Book.* New York: HarperCollins, 2009.

This edition pairs Margaret Wise Brown's classic, lyrical text with big, bold illustrations of adorable babies by Karen Katz.

Literacy bit: "Don't be afraid of the more advanced vocabulary in this book! Babies and young children need to hear vocabulary that is more advanced than the words they hear in everyday conversation in order to develop their language skills."

7 Butler, John. *Who Says Woof?* New York: Viking, 2003.

In this simple guessing-game story, the text asks which animal says a sound, and the next page shows a picture of an adorable baby animal.

Literacy bit: "Books like this one build children's confidence by inviting them to be active participants!"

8 Bynum, Janie. *Kiki's Blankie.* New York: Sterling, 2009.

Kiki the monkey won't go anywhere without her blankie, even in her dreams.

Literacy bit: "A sense of security is an important foundation for learning. Children who are stressed do not learn as well."

9 Cartwright, Reg. *What We Do.* New York: Henry Holt, 2004.

Simple text introduces animals and their activities. Because one animal is presented on each page, this book is easy to shorten as needed.

Literacy bit: "Reading about the natural world is an important way for children to gain an understanding of the animal and plant life around us, especially as we have fewer everyday experiences of nature in our modern world."

10 Cousins, Lucy. *Maisy Dresses Up*. Cambridge, MA: Candlewick, 1999.

Maisy the mouse has been invited to a costume party and needs to find a costume. With brief text and bright, bold illustrations, this is a great read-aloud.

Literacy bit: "During the toddler and preschool years, imaginary play will be an important way that your child explores and understands his world."

11 Fox, Mem. *Ten Little Fingers and Ten Little Toes*. New York: Houghton Mifflin, 2008.

With charming illustrations by Helen Oxenbury, this lovely little book celebrates babies around the world.

Literacy bit: "Though we often talk in broad terms about benchmarks for child development, it's important to remember that every child develops at her own pace and that children may develop at different rates in different areas."

12 Frederick, Heather Vogel. *Hide and Squeak*. New York: Simon and Schuster Books for Young Readers, 2011.

While a baby mouse tries to avoid bedtime, his father plays a game of hide-and-squeak.

Literacy bit: "When playing peekaboo or hide-and-seek, a young child is experimenting with the idea that people or objects still exist when he can't see them, but is also acting out the tension between a desire for independence and a desire for security."

13 Garcia, Emma. *Tip Tip Dig Dig*. New York: Sterling, 2007.

This big, bold book with brief text and chunky illustrations explores a construction site. After reading the text, revisit each machine and its movement. Encourage caregivers to interact with their children as follows:

> *Digger:* imitate digging in the ground
>
> *Mixer:* hold child and twist gently
>
> *Crane:* lift child into the air
>
> *Dump truck:* hold child firmly and tip her sideways (or upside down, for the more adventurous!)
>
> *Bulldozer:* move child forward in front of you
>
> *Road roller:* roll child gently on floor (for very young babies, roll arms or legs gently instead)

Literacy bit: "Playful interactions like these in the context of a story not only help your child's understanding of the content but also make reading a fun activity. This increases your child's desire to learn to read as he grows."

14 Hodgman, Ann. *Do Touch! Don't Touch!* **Wilton, CT: Tiger Tales, 2012.**

A baby learns about what is safe to touch and what is dangerous. Teach caregivers the signs YES and NO, and demonstrate how to use them to emphasize safe behavior as you read the story.

> *Literacy bit:* "Using sign language with young children to emphasize safety behavior gives a visual cue that helps children understand and even helps them outwardly monitor their own behavior. If you use these signs regularly, you may even see your child stop short and sign NO instead of touching something she shouldn't!"

15 Hodgman, Ann. *Uh-Oh! Oh No!* **Wilton, CT: Tiger Tales, 2012.**

Baby's in his high chair, all ready for breakfast, but spilled milk leads to lots of "uh-ohs" in this large-enough-for-storytime board book. And just when Daddy gets the mess all sorted out, it's time for . . . applesauce. Babies will enjoy the simple structure and infectious refrain of "Uh-oh! Oh no!"

> *Literacy bit:* "Babies look to caregivers' reactions to guide their own. If a parent seems confident that a booster shot or day-care drop-off is not a big deal, then the baby is less likely to melt down."

16 Hubbell, Patricia. *Pots and Pans.* **New York: HarperCollins, 1998.**

Baby makes a clatter and a bang playing with the pots and pans in this rhythmic, rhyming story. Follow up by letting kids and caregivers make their own kitchen band: provide each child with a plastic storage container (*much* less noisy than a roomful of pots and pans!) and a wooden spoon to play as a drum. Play some marching band music and invite everyone to drum along.

> *Literacy bit:* "Babies learn about the world through their senses! By the age of four months, babies begin to understand that sounds have meaning. Allowing them to experiment with sound allows for a full-body experience of rhythm, which is an important building block for understanding the rhythms of language."

17 Isadora, Rachel. *Peekaboo Morning*. New York: Putnam, 2002.

An African American toddler plays peekaboo, finding Mommy, Daddy, a bunny, a friend, and more.

> *Literacy bit:* "Starting at around six months of age, babies begin to understand that something still exists even if they can't see it. That's why peekaboo is so popular with babies at this age!"

18 Isadora, Rachel. *Uh-Oh!* New York: Harcourt, 2008.

An adorable toddler runs into a series of "uh-ohs," from a food dish on her head to Grandpa falling asleep during storytime. The book is cleverly set up and humorously delivered, with the giggling toddler enjoying every mess thoroughly. Extremely brief text and funny pictures tell the story.

> *Literacy bit:* "Reading about everyday experiences helps children develop text-to-self connection. After reading a book like this, refer to it in your everyday interactions with your child to reinforce those connections."

19 Katz, Karen. *The Babies on the Bus*. New York: HarperCollins, 2011.

This baby-friendly version of "The Wheels on the Bus" features Katz's trademark bright-eyed babies. Encourage caregivers to bounce babies in their laps as you sing the text together.

> *Literacy bit:* "The bouncing rhythm of this song and the accompanying movement help babies develop an understanding of the rhythm of language with their whole bodies!"

20 Katz, Karen. *Counting Kisses*. New York: Simon and Schuster, 2001.

Baby's family counts down to bedtime from ten little kisses on teeny-tiny toes to one last kiss on a sleepy, dreamy head. Reinforce the numbers in the story with large numbers on the flannelboard as you read the book, and invite caregivers to give the babies the appropriate number of kisses.

> *Literacy bit:* "Children learn counting, both forward and backward, through repetition and application of numbers to everyday experiences."

21 Katz, Karen. *Mommy Hugs*. New York: Simon and Schuster, 2006.

A mother and child count hugs throughout the day, from one "nuzzle-wuzzle wake-up hug" to ten good-night hugs.

> *Literacy bit:* "As you read to your child, make explicit connections between the events in the story and your child's daily life. This association enhances understanding and text-to-self connection."

22 Katz, Karen. *Ten Tiny Babies*. New York: Simon and Schuster, 2008.

One tiny baby starts to run, and one by one, her friends join her as they play, bathe, and settle down to bed. With large, bold illustrations and a predictable rhyming text, this is a great read-aloud.

> *Literacy bit:* "There is a reason why there are so many counting books for young children: though we often forget it, the names of the numbers are random words that must be said in a certain order. The best way to learn this skill is through constant repetition."

23 Larrañaga, Ana Martin. *Pepo and Lolo and the Red Apple*. Cambridge, MA: Candlewick, 2004.

Pepo, a pig, and Lolo, a chick, are determined to get the red apple hanging from a branch. With a little cooperation, they figure out how to get the yummy apple so they can share a snack.

> *Literacy bit:* "Simple, straightforward stories like this one help children develop a sense of logical sequencing and story structure."

24 Lewison, Wendy Cheyette. *Raindrop, Plop!* New York: Viking, 2004.

A little girl goes out to play in the rain as the rhyming text counts up from one to ten raindrops, then back down again. To add a sensory experience for babies, pass out small medicine droppers and cups of water to all the adults, and ask them to gently drop the correct number of drops onto their babies' heads or arms each time you read the number of raindrops. Pass out tissues to dry off afterward. For a drier version of this activity, pass out beanbags for the caregivers to gently drop onto their babies' laps each time a raindrop plops.

> *Literacy bit:* "Babies learn first about the world through touch, so using tactile sensations while presenting new information is a great way to reinforce a concept. Try repeating this activity later by counting soft blocks as you touch them to your baby, or even kisses!"

25 Martin, Bill Jr. *Brown Bear, Brown Bear, What Do You See?* New York: Henry Holt, 1967.

With large, bright pictures and a simple, repetitive text, this book is simply made for storytime. Add a new twist to this storytime favorite by teaching the signs for the animals in the story.

> *Literacy bit:* "Because the muscles required to sign develop earlier than those required to speak, most children can communicate by signing before they can speak clearly. Some babies sign as young as four months, while most children don't say their first words until closer to twelve months of age. The enhanced interaction that comes when a baby can express himself through signing leads to more quality language experiences."

26 McDonnell, Flora. *Splash!* Cambridge, MA: Candlewick, 1999.

Tiger is hot, Rhinoceros is hot, and Mama Elephant is hot. Luckily, Baby Elephant has the great idea to take everyone down to the watering hole for a splash! With oversized, bright pictures and a simple, vibrant text, this book is great for baby storytimes. Use a spray bottle to gently spray babies and caregivers with water when the animals splash.

Literacy bit: "Incorporating natural elements like water into stories increases engagement and helps babies fully understand concepts."

27 McGee, Marni. *Sleepy Me!* Intercourse, PA: Good Books, 2011.

A bear prepares for bed in this gentle board book. The larger format and bright colors make it great for storytime sharing, and the simple, lulling text is great for cuddling.

Literacy bit: "Stories that reinforce familiar routines help your baby feel more secure and can ease transitional times—like bedtime—that can often be stressful for babies."

28 McGee, Marni. *Wake Up, Me!* New York: Simon and Schuster, 2002.

Bouncy rhyming text and large pictures follow a toddler as he starts his day.

Literacy bit: "Everyday routines help children feel safe and secure and allow learning to happen more easily. Talking to your child about your routines as you go about them helps her to label and understand her experience."

29 McLean, Janet, and Andrew McLean. *Let's Go, Baby-o!* East Melbourne, Victoria, Australia: Allen and Unwin, 2011.

Beautiful pictures and simple text show a family truly moving through their day. For a real crowd pleaser, incorporate the movements while reading the book.

Literacy bit: "Movement helps the brain function! That's why, for many people, the act of taking longhand notes helps them remember concepts—the movement of the writing itself stimulates the brain and fixes the information in memory. For babies and young children, you can achieve the same effect through movement or signing."

30 McQuinn, Anna. *Lola Loves Stories.* Watertown, MA: Charlesbridge, 2010.

Each time Lola reads a story, she finds a way to extend it into her play, by dressing up, building things, or making something cool!

Literacy bit: "In this story, we see Lola extending her favorite stories into other activities. You can easily do the same for your child by incorporating favorite settings into play, providing simple objects to dress up like the characters, or using favorite book phrases in everyday interactions. These activities help young children develop concept knowledge, reinforce new vocabulary, and encourage imagination."

31 Meyers, Susan. *This Is the Way a Baby Rides.* New York: Abrams, 2005.

On a picnic with his parents, a baby bounces, rides, runs, jumps, and hides, in imitation of the baby animals he sees.

Literacy bit: "Babies and young children learn about the world through their senses, so it makes sense that animals and their sounds are some of the first things we teach young children. Animals are a festival for the senses—with noises to hear, interesting body parts to see, and sometimes even interesting textures to touch. When you describe your child's sensory experience with animals, you are helping him develop vocabulary that will be applied in all areas of life."

32 **Miller, Virginia.** *Ten Red Apples.* **Cambridge, MA: Candlewick, 2002.**

Bartholomew Bear explores many ways to play with his apple tree, from swinging from its branches to counting the apples. A side panel on each spread counts the apples from one to ten as you read the story. Read the story first, then go back and count the apples. Repeat the counting with apples on the flannelboard.

> *Literacy bit:* "Counting in the context of stories or real-world activities helps your baby internalize numbers."

33 **Murphy, Mary.** *How Kind!* **Cambridge, MA: Candlewick, 2002.**

Hen gives Pig an egg, which sets off a chain of kindnesses around the barnyard in this bold and bright picture book.

> *Literacy bit:* "Though it might sometimes seem a little boring to adults, repetition is key to how young children learn. Stories like this one reinforce key concepts and vocabulary through repetition. So when your child requests the same story over and over again, she's not trying to make you crazy, she's just trying to build her brain!"

34 **Nichols, Grace.** *Whoa, Baby, Whoa!* **New York: Bloomsbury, 2011.**

Baby just wants to see what's happening in the world, but his family keeps getting in the way when he tries to see what's cooking in the kitchen, climb up to get the books on the top shelf, or grab Grandpa's glasses—all to the constant refrain of "Whoa, Baby, whoa!" Each time, the rescuing family member explains why the blocked behavior is dangerous in simple, baby-friendly language. Finally, Baby decides to take some steps on his own, and his family cheers him on.

> *Literacy bit:* "Once babies are walking, they want to see the world! Even though we can't always let them do everything they want, reading stories like this one lets babies know that we understand their frustration!"

35 **O'Connell, Rebecca.** *The Baby Goes Beep.* **Brookfield, CT: Roaring Brook Press, 2003.**

A baby enjoys making sounds throughout the day, from beeping his imaginary car horn to shushing at bedtime.

> *Literacy bit:* "Phonological awareness is an important pre-literacy skill. It means the ability to hear and manipulate smaller sounds within words. When babies babble, they are experimenting with the sounds they hear others making. These are the building blocks of speech. Books like this one encourage children to play with familiar sounds."

36 **Oxenbury, Helen.** *Tickle, Tickle.* **New York: Macmillan, 1987.**

With brief rhyming text that invites participation and appealing, simple illustrations of a multiethnic group of babies, this large-format board book is perfect for storytime sharing. Encourage caregivers to act out the text with their babies as you read.

> *Literacy bit:* "When you act out the words of a story with your child, you make the story more fun for your child, but you also engage all his senses and help him understand and retain the vocabulary."

37 **Patricelli, Leslie.** *Faster! Faster!* **Sommerville, MA: Candlewick, 2012.**

A day at the park and a ride on Daddy's back turns into an adventure as the baby goes faster and faster—even as fast as a cheetah!

> *Literacy bit:* "By being willing to enter into the world of your child's imagination, you will enhance bonding and the quality of interactions with your child, which in turn enhances language skills."

38 **Perrin, Martine.** *Cock-a-Doodle Who?* **Chicago: Whitman, 2012.**

Simple rhyming text, along with pictures created from patterns and silhouettes, distinguishes this tale of animals around the farm.

> *Literacy bit:* "Books that feature high-contrast illustrations, especially in black and white, are perfect for the youngest babies, whose eyesight is still developing."

39 **Rylant, Cynthia.** *Brownie and Pearl Go for a Spin.* **New York: Beach Lane Books, 2012.**

Simple text and bold pictures tell the tale of all the places Brownie and Pearl travel to in their car.

> *Literacy bit:* "As a baby grows, her world gradually expands to include places in the community. Reading about those places enhances a young child's sense of security and understanding of her place within in the community."

40 **Scott, Ann Herbert.** *On Mother's Lap.* **New York: McGraw-Hill, 1972.**

Michael, a little Inuit boy, loves rocking on his mother's lap and wants to bring all his favorite things along—but he's not sure there is room for the baby, too. But he learns that there is always room for everyone on Mother's lap.

> *Literacy bit:* "Stories with cumulative or repetitive structure help children develop prediction skills."

41 Spinelli, Eileen. *Bath Time*. New York: Cavendish Children's Books, 2003.

A child fills up his bath with so many toys that there is no room for him in it.

> *Literacy bit:* "Reading stories about everyday activities helps children develop text-to-self connection. You can make this connection even more explicit by telling your child stories in which he is the main character. Such stories needn't be elaborate—young children love to hear descriptions of their everyday routines with themselves as the heroes."

42 Tafolla, Carmen. *Fiesta Babies*. Berkeley, CA: Tricycle Press, 2010.

Babies enjoy a Latino fiesta, including a parade, music, a siesta, and lots of hugs and kisses. The simple, bouncy text incorporates Spanish words. After you read the story, pass out maracas or shaking eggs and ask the caregivers to shake along to the rhythm of the text as you read it (or a few pages of it) again. Follow up with Latino music, and let the babies shake the maracas.

> *Literacy bit:* "In the first years of life, babies' brains are developing at an astounding rate—one thousand trillion synapses, or nerve connections, form in the first eight months alone. Around the age of twelve months, the brain begins pruning away unused connections so it will work more efficiently. This is why young children can pick up other languages so easily—their brains are more flexible than adults' brains. Exposing your child to other languages helps strengthen those neural connections so that they won't be pruned away."

43 Tafuri, Nancy. *All Kinds of Kisses*. New York: Little, Brown, 2012.

A series of baby animals all get kisses from their mothers in this made-for-storytime picture book, which features large, bright pictures and text that is easy to shorten if needed. Encourage caregivers to kiss their babies throughout and imitate the animal sounds.

> *Literacy bit:* "Cuddling and kissing encourage bonding and give your baby a sense of security. Cuddling as you read gives your child pleasurable associations with reading that can last a lifetime."

44 Tafuri, Nancy. *The Busy Little Squirrel*. New York: Simon and Schuster, 2007.

A little squirrel is too busy to nibble a pumpkin with Mouse, rest on a branch with Bird, or hop rocks with Frog. With large, colorful illustrations and a simple, repetitive text, this is a terrific storytime read-aloud. Reinforce the patterns and concepts in the story with this follow-up activity:

Introduce a squirrel puppet and ask it questions following the pattern of the story, but using the children's names. For example, ask, "Will you jump up and down with Katie?" "Will you clap your hands with Ethan?" Make the squirrel shake its head each time and explain that it is too busy preparing for winter. Then end with the squirrel asleep in your lap.

> *Literacy bit:* "Following up the story with an activity that includes each child by name increases text-to-self connection, encouraging babies to experience stories at a deeper level. The follow-up activity also reinforces the pattern of the story."

45 **Tafuri, Nancy. *Five Little Chicks*. New York: Simon and Schuster, 2006.**

Five little chicks try to find something to eat, until their mama shows them how to scratch for corn in this rhythmic, rhyming story.

> *Literacy bit:* "Read with expression and rhythm to help your child internalize the rhythms of language as you read."

46 **Tafuri, Nancy. *Mama's Little Bears*. New York: Scholastic, 2002.**

Three curious little bears wander away from their mama and get in trouble, but she's always nearby to give them a great big hug.

> *Literacy bit:* "From about the age of twelve months on, babies become very interested in exploring their environment and asserting their independence. Like the bears in the story, though, they still need to know that a caring adult is nearby."

47 **Thompson, Lauren. *Mouse's First Fall*. New York: Simon and Schuster, 2006.**

Mouse and his sister Minka play in the leaves in this simple picture book.

> *Literacy bit:* "Books like this one introduce science concepts such as seasons and weather in a way that focuses on the senses, and so are perfectly adapted to how young children learn."

48 **Walsh, Melanie. *My Nose, Your Nose*. Boston: Houghton Mifflin, 2002.**

Through simple text and large, colorful illustrations, this book explores the way that babies around the world are different, but ultimately the same.

> *Literacy bit:* "Young children learn through sensory experiences, so books and activities that employ comparison and contrast are ideal."

49 **Walton, Rick. *What Do We Do with the Baby?* New York: HarperCollins, 2008.**

A bouncy, rhythmic text details all the things you can do with a baby, from hugging and kissing to bouncing, tickling toes, and playing peekaboo. Encourage caregivers to join in as you read!

Literacy bit: "Books like this one encourage interaction with your baby! Don't just read the book—use funny voices, stop and point out interesting things on the pages, and ask your child questions even if she is too little to respond. Engaging interactions around books lay the foundation for a lifelong love of reading and facility with language."

50 Weeks, Sarah. *Overboard!* New York: Harcourt, 2006.

From morning to night, a baby bunny likes to throw everything overboard, from the food on his tray to the stuffed animals in his crib. Bouncy rhyming text and bold illustrations make this book terrific for storytime sharing, and it's a great discussion starter for caregivers on how they deal with this universal phenomenon.

Literacy bit: "Somewhere between six and nine months of age, babies become junior scientists. They conduct experiments to see what will happen when they drop or throw things—and they like to perform many, many tests! This is all part of how children develop an understanding of the world and its properties through play."

51 Wells, Rosemary. *Carry Me!* New York: Hyperion, 2006.

A little bunny tells, in lyrical rhyming text, how he yearns for his parents to interact with him. This book is perfect for baby storytimes, as it provides beautiful illustrations and lovely text for babies but also sneakily works in early literacy tips for grown-ups. Try structuring a baby program around the book (this would be especially appropriate for a one-time or introductory outreach program). Read the first section, "Carry Me!", then share a series of lap bounces and tickles. Next, read the second section, "Talk to Me!", and follow it up with fingerplays and rhymes. Last, read "Sing to Me!" and end your program with songs and music play.

Literacy bit: "Books, songs, bounces, and rhymes are important for developing early literacy, but they only work because of *you!* Interaction with a caring adult is the most important factor in developing early literacy skills, self-regulation, and emotional security."

52 Wild, Margaret. *Itsy-Bitsy Babies.* Prahran, Victoria, Australia: Little Hare Books, 2009.

The itsy-bitsy babies all like different things, from clapping to going to town to banging on drums—but they all love hugs. With simple rhyming text and bright illustrations by Jan Ormerod, this is a great storytime read-aloud, with lots of actions to go with the story.

Literacy bit: "Make books come alive for your baby by acting out the text. This not only makes the story more fun but helps your baby fully understand the meaning of the words."

53 Wild, Margaret. *Kiss Kiss!* New York: Simon and Schuster Books for Young Readers, 2003.

Baby Hippo is in such a rush to play that he forgets to kiss his mama, but all the animals in the jungle remind him.

> *Literacy bit:* "This story is a great example of using specific and descriptive words that children understand. When you use these words with your child, you build vocabulary and understanding."

Choral Reading

Choral reading simply means a group of people are reading aloud together. In baby storytime, this means that each caregiver holds a copy of the book and the librarian leads the reading. Reading aloud teaches babies about communication and introduces stories to them in a fun way. While the librarian is reading, the caregivers can follow along and point out words, shapes, colors, and pictures on the page. This activity allows babies to touch the book and make associations with the words being read by the librarian. Reading aloud also teaches babies listening, memory, and vocabulary skills, while allowing them to gain information about the world around them. Caregivers may feel more comfortable reading aloud, using silly voices, and so forth, when it is done in a group. When the adults all read aloud together, the babies will often become quiet, fascinated with the deliberate sound of so many voices in unison. Most important of all, however, the choral reading technique emphasizes the highest goal of baby storytime: interaction between child and caregiver.

Some suggested books for choral reading follow.

54 Broach, Elise. *Seashore Baby*. New York: Little, Brown, 2010.

A baby spends a day at the beach in this bright lift-the-flap book.

> *Literacy bit:* "As you read with your child, don't just plow ahead with the text. Take time to point out the pictures and ask questions, and give your child time to process and answer. Adults tend to expect children to answer questions in just a few seconds, but young children need much longer than that to understand the question and process their answers. Think of the time you give your child in these interactions as a gift of your attention."

55 Dewdney, Anna. *Llama Llama Hoppity-Hop*. New York: Penguin, 2012.

Llama Llama claps, jumps, stretches, and moves in this rhyming board book.

> *Literacy bit:* "Movement stimulates the brain! When your baby is introduced to language in the context of movement, he is more likely to understand and retain the vocabulary."

56 Janovitz, Marilyn. *Play Baby Play!* **Naperville, IL: Sourcebooks, 2012.**

Smiling babies congregate at playgroup to read stories, ring bells, and roll around together.

> *Literacy bit:* "From about the age of twelve months, children become very interested in other children, even if they don't quite know how to interact with them. Stories like this one provide a model for social interaction and help babies understand their own experiences."

57 London, Jonathan. *Snuggle Wuggle.* **New York: Red Wagon, 2002.**

A series of animals give different kinds of hugs in this simple board book.

> *Literacy bit:* "Repetitive structures like the one in this book help young children develop confidence and prediction skills."

58 Murphy, Mary. *I Kissed the Baby.* **Cambridge, MA: Candlewick, 2003.**

The animals in the barnyard delight in kissing, tickling, and otherwise playing with the new duckling. This book uses strong black-and-white contrast with splashes of color, perfect for little eyes, and the strongly rhythmic text makes a wonderful, bouncy read-aloud.

> *Literacy bit:* "In the first six to nine months of life, a baby's vision is slowly developing. Babies can see strong contrasts best, so books with bold black-and-white shapes, like this one, are ideal."

59 Tracy, Tom. *Show Me!* **New York: Harper, 1999.**

A mother nuzzles her baby's nose, tweaks his cheek, and more in this brief board book.

> *Literacy bit:* "Eye contact is extremely important for bonding and attention, especially in the first few months of life when a baby can't see more than a few feet. Make sure you put your face close to your baby's when you are interacting."

60 Wells, Rosemary. *Shopping.* **New York: Penguin, 2009.**

Part of the Baby Max and Ruby series, this simple board book story tells of Max and Ruby's trip to the grocery store in bouncy rhyming text.

> *Literacy bit:* "Books that mirror the everyday experiences of babies help them make sense of the world and develop a great sense of security. Without a feeling of security, children cannot learn as effectively."

4

Rhymes and Songs

· ·

RHYMES AND SONGS are a vital component of baby storytimes. Music stimulates the left side of a baby's brain, helping develop creativity and expression. The movement activities that often accompany music stimulate neural networks, helping young children to cement new experiences in their minds. Songs and rhymes introduce new vocabulary in context, and the way that words are broken up in songs helps children understand syllables. And, at a practical level, nothing soothes a noisy baby like the sound of the human voice singing or chanting rhythmically.

Whether you think you can sing or not, we encourage you to sing with your own voice in baby storytimes rather than relying on prerecorded music. The interaction that accompanies live singing is crucial to early language development, and caregivers are much more likely to chime in and sing along if you sing yourself. If you are nervous about your singing voice, select well-known children's songs for your programs so that the caregivers will sing along more readily. And remember, babies are the most accepting audience in the world—they don't care if you're sharp or flat. They just love to hear you sing!

61 Baby Hugs

Baby has a head,
Baby has a nose,
Baby even has ten little toes.
Shake your little head.
Touch your little nose.
Wiggle, wiggle ten little toes.
Baby has ears,
Baby has a tummy,
Baby even has a happy mommy.
Wiggle your ears,
Tickle your tummy,
Give a big hug to your mommy!

> *Literacy bit:* "Children learn best when they feel safe and loved. Cuddly rhymes like this one reduce stress and help your child develop mental resilience."

62 Baby in the Mirror (to the tune of "My Bonnie Lies Over the Ocean")

Pass out small mirrors to caregivers to use during this song.

Oh, who is that baby in the mirror?
Oh, who is that baby I see?
Oh, who is that baby in the mirror?
Who's that looking back at me?
Baby, baby, that's my sweet baby I see!
Baby, baby, come on and smile for me!

> *Literacy bit:* "Babies love looking into mirrors! Doing so helps them develop the muscles in their eyes that will later be used to track text on a page. Mirror watching also helps babies begin to learn about themselves."

63 The Baby Is Trying to Sleep

The chicks say, "Cheep, cheep,"
The puppies say, "Woof, woof,"
The mommies say, "Shhh, shhh, the baby is trying to sleep."
The birds say, "Tweet, tweet,"
The kittens say, "Meow, meow,"
The daddies say, "Shhh, shhh, the baby is trying to sleep."

> *Literacy bit:* "Between three and six months of age, most babies begin babbling in single syllables, such as 'bah.' Between six and nine months, most babies start putting syllables together (for example, 'bah-bah'). Between nine and twelve months, babies' babbling usually starts to sound more like speech, even if you

don't understand the words yet. Though we don't always recognize it as a baby's first attempts to speak, that's exactly what babbling is!"

64 Bath Time

Run the water, *(mime turning on faucet)*
Shut the door, *(mime closing door)*
Get the ducky, *(mime picking up rubber duck)*
Cross the floor. *(walk fingers of one hand over the palm of the other)*

Water off, *(mime turning off faucet)*
Here I come, *(hold hands out in "ta-da" gesture)*
Wash me up, *(gently scrub baby)*
Oh what fun!

> *Literacy bit:* "Narrating events in your child's daily life will help him learn sequencing skills. As your child gets older, ask him to tell you a story about a simple event, such as taking a bath."

65 Bathtime Fun

Rub-a-dub-dub, three kids in a tub
And what do you think they do?
They wash, they play,
They splash away,
And then they dry off too!

> *Literacy bit:* "Sharing a silly rhyme like this one brings more playfulness to your interactions with your child and helps babies adapt during transitional times such as bath time or diaper changes."

66 Bonjour Song: A Song in French (to the tune of "Happy Birthday")

Bonjour les enfants! (bon-JOOR lays ahn-fahn)
Bonjour les enfants!
Comment ça va? (ka-mohn sah vah)
Bien, merci. (byen, mare-SEE)

Hello, children!
Hello, children!
How are you?
I'm fine, thank you.

> *Literacy bit:* "Babies can understand sounds in many languages, but when the brain begins to prune synaptic connections around the age of one year, this ability decreases. Exposing your baby to other languages in the early years will make it easier for her to learn those languages later in life."

67 Building a Snowman

I'm going to build a snowman, big and round. *(hold arms out)*
I'll start by rolling snow from the ground. *(pretend to roll the snow)*
First I'll make his body: one, two, three. *(count on fingers)*
Then I'll add his nose and eyes, so he can see. *(point to nose and eyes)*
Last I'll add a bit of magic, so he'll come to life at night. *(blow in hand like spreading magic dust)*
I'll put a top hat on his head; now he looks just right! *(pat head)*

> *Literacy bit:* "Acting out rhymes helps your child learn about size and shape. You can also develop your baby's vocabulary about these concepts by comparing the sizes and shapes of objects around the house."

68 Busy Squirrel

Up the tree and down again, *(point up, then down)*
The busy squirrel looks for his friend. *(look all around)*
Fall is coming, don't you know?
We have to prepare for the winter snow. *(shiver)*
They've been burying acorns for weeks and weeks. *(mime burying acorns)*
Now they need to find them and stuff them in their cheeks! *(puff out cheeks)*

> *Literacy bit:* "Ask questions! Relate rhymes and books to the child's experiences. Use rhymes like this one as a springboard to discuss things you and your child have seen."

69 Going Out on Four

I put on my hat, *(touch baby's head)*
And slip on my shoes. *(point to baby's shoes)*
I wiggle my fingers, *(wiggle fingers)*
And count to two. *(put up two fingers)*
I put on my mittens, *(mime pulling mittens on baby)*
And point at the door. *(point at door)*
I tap my toes, *(tap baby's toes)*
And count to four. *(count to four on fingers)*

> *Literacy bit:* "Counting in rhymes and other everyday routines helps your child develop mathematical thinking."

70 I Can Zoo

Perform the sounds and actions indicated.

I can roar like a lion,
I can growl like a bear,
Like a monkey I can swing my arms high in the air.

I can trumpet like an elephant,
I can hiss like a snake,
Like a peacock I can give my tail a shake, shake, shake.
I can hoot like an owl,
I can buzz like a bee,
Like a giraffe I can stretch my neck high in the tree.
I can munch like a panda,
I can snap like a croc,
Like a turtle I can warm myself sitting on a rock.

> *Literacy bit:* "Action rhymes help develop small and large muscles that will later enable your child to crawl, walk, and feed himself."

71 I Wish I Was a Fish

Teach the sign FISH, then move the sign around as indicated in the rhyme.

I wish wish wish
I was a fish fish fish.
I'd swim down low,
Then jump up high,
Then splash back down,
Oh my oh my!
I'd swim left and I'd swim right
Through the day and through the night.
I'd wiggle through the water
With a splish splash splish
If I was a little fish!

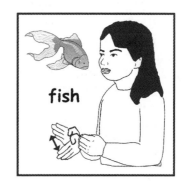

fish

> *Literacy bit:* "American Sign Language (ASL) is a real language that is expressed with the hands and face instead of the mouth. Exposing your child to even basic ASL stimulates her language development just as much as exposure to speech."

72 I'm a Big Kid

I'm a big kid,
Can't you see?
I can use the potty
Just like Mommy!
I'm a big kid.
Look at me!
I can use the potty
Just like Daddy!

> *Literacy bit:* "New skills take time to master. Each child develops at his own pace, so show encouragement but let your child take the lead."

73 I'm Sick

I was sick all day today, *(make a sad face)*
I sneezed and coughed and couldn't play! *(pretend to sneeze)*
My mommy gave me lots of love, *(give yourself a hug)*
Special medicine and sweet things to dream of. *(pretend to sleep)*
When I woke up I was feeling great *(stretch arms)*
And I was well enough to have my playdate! *(cheer)*

> *Literacy bit:* "A secure environment helps your child develop trust. That sense of security will give her the courage to explore the world and eventually become more independent."

74 Little Duck

I'm a duck, a little yellow duck,
And I say "quack-quack-quack."
I'm a duck, a little yellow duck,
With feathers on my back. *(tickle baby's back)*

> *Literacy bit:* "Make up silly rhymes and encourage your baby to imitate the words and sounds he hears. This helps your child develop phonological awareness, or an understanding of the smaller parts of words."

75 Little Turtle: A Scarf Rhyme

Let the child lie on the floor and cover her face with a see-through scarf. When the turtle pops out to say hello, lift the scarf with an expression of surprise. Older babies and toddlers can hold the scarves themselves during this rhyme.

Here's a little turtle, hiding in his shell.
Here's a little turtle that we love so well.
He always moves slowly, he never moves fast,
Until he pops out to say hello at last!
Hello!

> *Literacy bit:* "Learning the concept of object permanence (the idea that the object is still there even when you can no longer see it) is an important developmental step. Babies test this idea through games like hide-and-seek and peekaboo. When young children understand object permanence, they become more confident in themselves and in the idea that parents or caregivers may go away but they will come back."

76 Peekaboo

Peekaboo, I see you.
Now I don't, and now I do.
I slip behind and there I hide.

Now I pop up, grinning wide.
Now I'm gone and now I'm here.
One side, other side, far and near.
I love to hide and so do you,
But I love most to say *peekaboo!*

> *Literacy bit:* "Each time you go out of sight and come back, you are teaching your child that you still exist when he can't see you. This lesson promotes a sense of security that is vital for learning."

77 **Picking Apples** (to the tune of "Skip to My Lou")

Picking apples from the tree, *(mime picking apples)*
Picking apples from the tree,
Picking apples from the tree,
Picking apples for you and me! *(point to child and self)*

> *Literacy bit:* "Singing helps young children develop language skills because it breaks words down into syllables, emphasizing the rhythm of the words."

78 **Roll the Ball** (to the tune of "Row, Row, Row Your Boat")

This song can be a large-group activity or a one-on-one activity between caregivers and children. If singing with a large group, have caregivers and babies sit in a circle and sing and roll to each baby in turn. For a one-on-one interaction, give each caregiver a ball and have her or him roll the ball to the baby as the whole group sings.

Roll, roll, roll the ball,
Happy as can be,
(Name) rolls it back to me,
Quick as one, two, three.

> *Literacy bit:* "The back-and-forth nature of this ball game imitates communication. We talk to our children, and, though we sometimes forget it, even the tiniest baby communicates with us too, through cries, grunts, gestures, and more. Developing effective communication with other people is your baby's most important job in the early years of life."

79 **Seed**

A tiny seed grew in the ground, *(hold up fist)*
With golden sunlight all around. *(wiggle fingers of other hand around fist)*
The rain fell down, *(wiggle fingers of other hand down over fist)*
The seed, it grew *(begin to open fist)*
And sprouted pretty flowers too! *(open fist all the way)*

> *Literacy bit:* "Rhymes like this one help children learn the smaller sounds in words, a necessary building block for reading."

80 **Sleigh Ride**

Give each caregiver a towel or small blanket to spread flat on the floor. Place baby on the towel or blanket, then lift one end and pull it to give baby a gentle sleigh ride. Play or sing "Jingle Bells" or "Sleigh Ride" as you do this.

> *Literacy bit:* "Engaging in playful moments with your child enhances bonding and security."

81 **Snowball**

Hand out scarves to each caregiver to use during the rhyme.

I pull on my mittens, *(pull scarf over baby's hands)*
On my head I put my hat. *(put scarf on baby's head)*
I toss on my scarf, *(fling scarf over baby's shoulder)*
And I'm out the door like that!
The snow is drifting down *(let scarf drift down to the floor in front of baby)*
To the ground just so.
I gather up a bunch of it *(ball up scarf between hands)*
And here's the snowball that I throw! *(throw the balled scarf gently at baby)*

> *Literacy bit:* "When you use scarves or other objects with rhymes, you give your child a multisensory experience of language."

82 **Snowflake Song** (to the tune of "Frère Jacques")

I like snowflakes, I like snowflakes,
In the air, in the air,
Whirling twirling snowflakes, whirling twirling snowflakes,
Everywhere, everywhere.

> *Literacy bit:* "Babies learn to associate words with things they see in the natural world. Point out objects as you talk to your baby through the day."

83 **Snowman Song** (to the tune of "I'm a Little Teapot")

I'm a little snowman, short and fat. *(hold hands out to indicate shape)*
Here is my scarf *(mime putting scarf on baby)*
And here is my hat. *(touch baby's head)*
When the snow is falling, come and play. *(wiggle fingers to represent snow falling)*
Sun comes out, I melt away. *(droop to floor)*

> *Literacy bit:* "Singing helps your child learn both vocabulary and rhythm."

84 **Springtime on the Farm** (to the tune of "Down on Grandpa's Farm")

It is spring, it is spring, springtime on the farm!
It is spring, it is spring, springtime on the farm!
Springtime on the farm, there is a new baby cow,
Springtime on the farm, there is a new baby cow.
The calf, he makes a sound like this: moo-moo!
The calf, he makes a sound like this: moo-moo!

Repeat with other animals, such as baby chick, piglet, lamb, or duckling.

> *Literacy bit:* "Imitating animal sounds helps your child make associations with the world around her and develop phonemic awareness."

85 **Sticker on My Knee** (to the tune of "If You're Happy and You Know It")

Give each caregiver a sticker to use during this song.

There's a sticker on my knee, on my knee.
There's a sticker on my knee, on my knee.
Oh, woe is me,
There's a sticker on my knee.
There's a sticker on my knee, on my knee.

There's a sticker on my head . . . Oh, how I dread . . .
There's a sticker on my arm . . . It's not doing any harm . . .
There's a sticker on my nose . . . Why do you suppose . . .
There's a sticker on my diaper . . . I don't want to be a griper . . .
There's a sticker on my tummy . . . Isn't it funny . . .

> *Literacy bit:* "Learning the words for body parts is an important step in vocabulary development, and it also helps babies learn that they are separate from their caregivers."

86 **Stinky Diaper** (to the tune of "Frère Jacques")

Stinky diaper, stinky diaper,
Changing time, changing time.
Let's take off the dirty one,
Let's put on a clean one.
Glad you're mine, glad you're mine.

> *Literacy bit:* "Singing just before and during stressful times—such as diaper changes—reduces stress and distracts your baby, making less frustration for caregivers."

87 Take Me Out to the Park (to the tune of "Take Me Out to the Ball Game")

Take me out to the park, *(sway baby side to side)*
Take me outside to play.
Green, green grass and the blue, blue sky, *(hold baby down low, then up high)*
And other kiddos go racing by.
Let me play, play, play in the sandbox,
Then push me in the swing.
For it's one, two, three swings I'm up *(swing baby gently back and forth)*
And that's why I sing!

> *Literacy bit:* "Children learn through play. If you give your child plenty of time for unstructured play, he will be learning important skills such as problem solving, vocabulary, and social skills."

88 Today I Feel . . .

Make the faces that go with each line.

Today I am happy, it's a beautiful day,
All of my friends were home and could play.
Today I am mad, I stomp and I pout,
And then I let loose with a scream and a shout!
Today I am sad, I just want to cry,
I had an accident and Mom let out a big sigh.
Today I feel silly, I'm laughing and giggling,
My daddy is tickling me and I can't stop wiggling.

> *Literacy bit:* "Young children can often feel overwhelmed by emotions they don't understand. Labeling your baby's emotions helps her understand what those feelings are. As your child gets older, acknowledging your child's emotions with statements like 'I can see that you are angry because you are kicking your feet' helps your child understand and process emotions."

89 Twinkle, Twinkle, Little Star (traditional)

Sign STAR while singing this favorite song. Pull out this activity anytime you need to calm and center the group. Because the adults know the song, they will generally sing along confidently, and the babies will be distracted and calmed by the sound of so many voices singing a familiar song.

Twinkle, twinkle, little star,
How I wonder what you are.
Up above the world so high,
Like a diamond in the sky.
Twinkle, twinkle, little star,
How I wonder what you are.

Literacy bit: "As we see in this activity, you don't need to know a lot of signs in order to sign with a song. The movement and the sound work together to calm your baby."

90 Two Little Blackbirds (adapted traditional)

Two little blackbirds sitting in the grass, *(sign BIRD)*
One named Slow and one named Fast. *(sign BIRD slowly, then quickly to match the names)*
Fly away, Slow! *(sign BIRD again, then make beak shape fly slowly across your body to one side; keep your hand there as you sign the next line)*
Fly away, Fast! *(sign BIRD with your other hand, then make it fly quickly across your body to the opposite side)*
Come back, Slow! *(bring first hand slowly back to your mouth)*
Come back, Fast! *(bring second hand quickly back to your mouth)*

Literacy bit: "Using sign language with young children can reduce frustration and enhance language skills. In this activity, we combine spoken words with signs, and we change the way we produce the signs to match whether the bird is slow or fast. This helps your baby understand the concepts in visual, auditory, and tactile ways. In addition, the cross-lateral motion (reaching your hand across your body) helps the two hemispheres of the brain communicate with one another."

91 Wake in the Morning

Wake in the morning, sing out my song.
Mommy comes into my room and sings along.
"Good morning, sweet baby, are you happy today?
Let's get you dressed so we can go play."
Diaper is changed and fresh clothes put on,
Then we go to the kitchen, with a small yawn.
We eat breakfast quickly and race outside,
Where we get to swing side by side.

> *Literacy bit:* "Even as a baby, your child is learning the sounds and rhythms of language, so sing and talk with your baby throughout the day."

5

Bounces and
Movement Activities

· ·

LAP BOUNCES ARE a traditional way of soothing a fussy baby, engaging an alert baby, and—although it has always been a hidden function of the activity—stimulating language development. In agrarian societies where large families were the norm, children learned the rhymes while watching parents or grandparents bounce baby brothers or sisters, and passed them on to their own children when they grew up. In today's world, with smaller families often living apart from grandparents and other relatives, many new parents may not have been exposed to these rhymes and techniques; thus repetition is just as important for the caregivers as for the children. Repeating favorite bounces week to week in your storytimes allows the adults to grow comfortable with them and increases the odds that they will use the bounces at home.

Adults should sit in a chair or on the floor with babies on their laps. Very young babies who cannot hold their heads up yet are often more comfortable lying along the caregiver's legs, facing the caregiver. Older babies can sit in the adult's lap, either facing the caregiver or looking out at the world.

92 **A-Bouncing We Will Go** (to the tune of "A-Hunting We Will Go")

A-bouncing we will go,
A-bouncing we will go,
Hi ho the derry-o,
A-bouncing we will go.

A-tickling we will go . . .
A-kissing we will go . . .

> *Literacy bit:* "When you sing while bouncing your child on your lap, you are actually helping her develop an understanding of the rhythms of speech!"

93 **Airplane Song** (to the tune of "A Bicycle Built for Two")

Hold the child in a football hold and gently move and sway him through the air along with the words.

Airplanes, airplanes
Flying through the air.
Flying up and flying down
All without a care.
Sometimes we bump around
Before we all touch down.
Then again we fly
Up in the sky
'Cause that's what airplanes do.

> *Literacy bit:* "Swaying activities like this one help children develop balance."

94 **Animal Bounce**

A horsey trots, a horsey trots, trot, trot, trot.
A horsey trots, a horsey trots, trot, trot, trot.
An elephant stomps, an elephant stomps, stomp, stomp, stomp.
An elephant stomps, an elephant stomps, stomp, stomp, stomp.
A mouse tiptoes, a mouse tiptoes, tip tip-toe.
A mouse tiptoes, a mouse tiptoes, tip tip-toe.
A birdie flies, a birdie flies, up and away!
A birdie flies, a birdie flies, up and away!

> *Literacy bit:* "Because babies learn about the world through their senses, whenever you can present opposites in a clear, fun way, you are helping your baby understand the world more clearly."

95 Animal Moves

This is the way the bunny hops: hop, hop, hop, hop.
This is the way the horsey trots: trit trot, trit trot.
This is the way the froggy jumps: jump, jump, jump, jump.
This is the way the birdie flies: fly away, fly away!

> *Literacy bit:* "Pretending to be animals and imitating their movements help your child's physical development."

96 Baby Love

Lovey dovey kissy cuddly, I bounce my baby slow,
Lovey dovey kissy cuddly, I bounce my baby low,
Lovey dovey kissy cuddly, I bounce my baby high.
I bounce and bounce until I stop, then lift baby to the sky!

> *Literacy bit:* "When babies feel loved and secure, they feel more confident to explore the world around them."

97 "Big Ship Sails" (from *Sharing Cultures with Ella Jenkins* by Ella Jenkins. Washington, DC: Smithsonian Folkways, 2003)

Let the babies ride in the boats of caregivers' laps as you play and sing this lilting song.

> *Literacy bit:* "There are many wonderful recordings of songs for young children, but you might notice that the best ones for babies tend to use the human voice with very little instrumentation. That's because babies are highly attuned to the sound of the human voice—and their caregivers' voices are their favorite sounds in the world!"

98 Bouncing Song (to the tune of "Skip to My Lou")

Bounce and bounce and bounce and *stop.*
Bounce and bounce and bounce and *stop.*
Bounce and bounce and bounce and *stop.*
Now bounce that baby right up to the top! *(lift baby up)*

Repeat slowly, then quickly.

> *Literacy bit:* "Make sure to pause after the *stop* in each line to build suspense! This blending of the expected continuation of the song with the unexpected pauses lays the foundation for humor (which is, after all, the collision of the expected and the unexpected). So don't be surprised if your baby reacts with giggles!"

99 Cracker Count

Teach the sign CRACKER and use it throughout this bounce.

One CRACKER, two CRACKERS,
Three CRACKERS, four.
Five CRACKERS, six CRACKERS,
Seven CRACKERS. More!
Eight CRACKERS, nine CRACKERS,
Ten CRACKERS. Then
Eat up all the CRACKERS and
Start again!
Let's count them slowly!
Let's count them quickly!

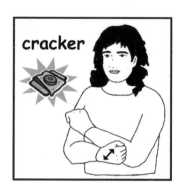

Literacy bit: "Teaching babies the signs for everyday objects allows them to communicate before they can speak clearly, which can reduce frustration for children and caregivers alike."

100 Fire Truck Song (to the tune of "Ten Little Indians"; adapted traditional)

Hurry, hurry, drive the fire truck.
Hurry, hurry, drive the fire truck.
Hurry, hurry, drive the fire truck.
Ding, ding, ding, ding, ding!

Hurry, hurry, raise the ladder. *(lift baby)*
Hurry, hurry, raise the ladder. *(lift baby)*
Hurry, hurry, raise the ladder. *(lift baby)*
Ding, ding, ding, ding, ding!

Hurry, hurry, put out the fire. *(jiggle baby gently)*
Hurry, hurry, put out the fire. *(jiggle baby gently)*
Hurry, hurry, put out the fire. *(jiggle baby gently)*
Ding, ding, ding, ding, ding!

Literacy bit: "Sharing rhymes and songs that tell stories will help your baby develop sequencing skills."

101 Food Bounce Song (to the tune of "On Top of Spaghetti")

If you were spaghetti, you'd wobble like this, *(jiggle baby gently)*
You'd wibble and wobble, and it would be bliss.
If you were hot water, and started to boil, *(bounce baby)*
You'd bounce all around, and it would be joy.
But if you were popcorn, you'd jump in the air. *(lift baby repeatedly into air)*
Pop pop pop pop pop pop! Pop everywhere!

BOUNCES AND MOVEMENT ACTIVITIES • 49

Literacy bit: "This is a great activity to redirect your child when she is fussy. Research shows that hearing a caregiver sing actually alters a baby's emotional state."

102 How Do You Move?

I can move like an inchworm, up and down, up and down. *(jiggle baby gently)*
I can bound like a squirrel, up and down, up and down. *(bounce baby more energetically)*
I can hop like a bunny, up and down, up and down. *(bounce baby high)*

> *Literacy bit:* "Simple rhymes such as this one give your child a whole-body experience of opposites."

103 How Many Miles to Dublin? (traditional)

How many miles to Dub-l-in?
Three score and ten.
Will we be there by candlelight?
Yes, and back again.
Hup, hup, my little horse,
Hup, hup, again.
Hup, hup, my little horse,
Hup, hup, again.

> *Literacy bit:* "Traditional rhymes like this one often contain vocabulary that you wouldn't use in everyday life. And that's fine, because children need to hear vocabulary in many different contexts."

104 I Like

I like to go fast, *(bounce baby quickly)*
I like to go slow, *(bounce baby slowly)*
I like to go up in the air just so! *(lift baby into the air)*

I like to go fast, *(bounce baby quickly)*
I like to go slow, *(bounce baby slowly)*
I like to go back and forth just so! *(rock baby from side to side)*

I like to go fast, *(bounce baby quickly)*
I like to go slow, *(bounce baby slowly)*
I like to snuggle up just so! *(cuddle baby close)*

> *Literacy bit:* "Narrative skills include being able to understand and tell stories. When you narrate events in your child's day, you help him build this skill."

105 If You're Bouncy (to the tune of "If You're Happy and You Know It")

If you're bouncy and you know it, give a bounce,
If you're bouncy and you know it, give a bounce,
If you're bouncy and you know it, then your bounce will surely show it,
If you're bouncy and you know it, give a bounce.

If you're wiggly and you know it . . .
If you're cuddly and you know it . . .

> *Literacy bit:* "When you bounce and sing to a song with a strong rhythm such as this one, your child both hears and feels the rhythms of spoken language."

106 Marching Flagpoles

Play "Stars and Stripes Forever" by John Philip Sousa while leading a parade. Invite caregivers to hold children upright in front of them like a flagpole, with their arms wrapped securely around the children's shoulders and hips. Direct caregivers to change movements as you move. Try dancing, tiptoeing, swaying the children, spinning slowly, walking slowly, and more.

> *Literacy bit:* "Marching, dancing, and swaying to music will help your child learn rhythm and internalize the rhythms of language."

107 My Bonnie Lies Over the Ocean (traditional)

My Bonnie lies over the ocean, *(sway from side to side during this verse)*
My Bonnie lies over the sea,
My Bonnie lies over the ocean,
Oh, bring back my Bonnie to me.

Bring back, bring back, *(lift child and bring her back on each line)*
Oh, bring back my Bonnie to me, to me.
Bring back, bring back,
Oh, bring back my Bonnie to me.

> *Literacy bit:* "When we add body movements to rhymes, we reinforce the child's understanding of concepts."

108 My Little White Mail Truck (to the tune of "Bumpin' Up and Down in My Little Red Wagon")

Bumpin' up and down in my little white mail truck. *(bounce baby in lap)*
Bumpin' up and down in my little white mail truck. *(bounce baby in lap)*
Bumpin' up and down in my little white mail truck. *(bounce baby in lap)*
Time to deliver the mail!

Open up the bag and deliver the letter. *(sway baby side to side)*
Open up the bag and deliver the letter. *(sway baby side to side)*
Open up the bag and deliver the letter. *(sway baby side to side)*
Time to deliver the mail!

Drop that letter into the mailbox. *(open legs so baby gently drops)*
Drop that letter into the mailbox. *(open legs so baby gently drops)*
Drop that letter into the mailbox. *(open legs so baby gently drops)*
Time to deliver the mail!

> *Literacy bit:* "Talking about jobs and people in your neighborhood helps your child learn about his community."

109 Pumpkin Bounce

Here's a little pumpkin bouncing on the vine. *(bounce baby gently)*
Roll it left *(sway to one side)*
And roll it right *(sway to the other side)*
And bounce it down the line. *(bounce)*

Here's a medium pumpkin bouncing on the vine. *(repeat, with slightly larger movements)*
Roll it left
And roll it right
And bounce it down the line.

Here's a great big pumpkin bouncing on the vine. *(repeat, with even larger movements)*
Roll it left
And roll it right
And bounce it down the line!

> *Literacy bit:* "When you adjust your voice and your movements to reflect the size of the pumpkin in the rhyme, you help your child understand the concepts of small, medium, and large with all her senses."

110 Ride, Ride: A Rhyme from Denmark (traditional)

The phrase "Ride, ride *ranke!*" in this traditional Danish bounce refers to the child bouncing in the caregiver's lap.

Ride, ride *ranke!*
Tell me where the road goes.
We will visit Grandpa.
Ride, ride *ranke!*

Ride, ride *ranke!*
And then when we descend,
We say, "Good day, good day!"
Ride, ride *ranke!*

Ride, ride *ranke!*
Grandma is so kind.
We can play what we want.
Ride, ride *ranke!*

Ride, ride *ranke!*
Now, galloping to Uncle's,
Is he home? Yes! Then stop!
Ride, ride *ranke!*

Ride, ride *ranke!*
Now the horse is tired.
The rider is full and glad,
Ride, ride *ranke!*

> *Literacy bit:* "Naming family members in rhymes reinforces the child's connection to his relatives, especially if he does not see them often. Feel free to replace the relatives' names in this rhyme with people who are meaningful to your child, such as Pop-Pop, Bubbe, or Uncle Tim."

111 **Rocket Song** (to the tune of "Pop Goes the Weasel")

(Name) is blasting off into space *(bounce child on lap)*
In a big red rocket.
First we count and then we blast off—
5, 4, 3, 2, 1! Blast off! *(pause bouncing during countdown)*

Roar goes the rocket. *(lift baby into the air)*

> *Literacy bit:* "Counting in rhymes and songs helps your baby internalize mathematical skills and sequencing."

112 **The Swing**

Play a recording of this song from *100 Sing-Along-Songs for Kids* (Franklin, TN: Cedarmont, 2007). This song is based on the classic poem by Robert Louis Stevenson, which is now in the public domain. Invite the caregivers to stand, holding their babies, and sway the babies through the air mimicking the motions of a swing as the song plays.

How do you like to go up in a swing,
Up in the air so blue?
Oh, I do think it the pleasantest thing
Ever a child can do!

Up in the air and over the wall
Till I can see so wide,
River and trees and cattle and all
Over the countryside.

Till I look down on the garden green,
Down on the roof so brown—
Up in the air I go flying again,
Up in the air and down!

Literacy bit: "Swaying stimulates the development of the proprioceptive system, which helps a child know where she is in space. School-age children who do not have a well-developed proprioceptive system often have difficulties concentrating."

113 Taking Turns Bounce

Teach the sign TAKE TURNS and then sign it as you bounce the child from side to side in this rhyme. See a video demonstration of this bounce at www.storytimestuff.net.

Taking turns is fun to do.
First it's me and then it's you.
Back and forth and to and fro.
Your turn, my turn, here we go!

Literacy bit: "Babies and toddlers live very much in the present, so the concept of waiting for a turn is difficult for them! The back-and-forth nature of this bounce and the sign TAKE TURNS both emphasize that the turn is coming. Use the sign TAKE TURNS in everyday interactions with your child to describe and cue desired behavior."

114 This Is the Way

This is the way the babies ride, jiggety-jog, jiggety-jog. *(bounce baby on lap)*
This is the way the firefighter rides, nee-naw, nee-naw. *(bounce baby more energetically)*
This is the way the postman rides, ride and stop, ride and stop! *(bounce and stop repeatedly)*

Literacy bit: "Sharing rhymes about people children may encounter helps them learn about their community."

115 Tick Tock

Swing baby gently back and forth while saying the rhyme.

Tick tock
Goes the clock.
Back and forth,
It never stops.
Tick tock
All day long
While we sing
Our clockwork song.
Tick tock
To and fro.
It's never "stop."
It's always "go."
Tick tock
All around.
But now the clock
Is winding . . . down.
Tick . . . tock . . .
Goes . . . the . . . clock
Until . . . it . . . comes . . .
To . . . a . . . *stop!*

Wind up the clock by tickling the baby's tummy and repeat the rhyme.

> *Literacy bit:* "Swaying your child helps stimulate the sensory receptors found in muscles, tendons, joints, and the inner ear, all of which detect the motion or position of the body. This action lays the foundation for the large and small muscle control needed to read and write."

116 Train Bounce

Choo choo, choo choo, riding on the train. *(bounce child)*
Choo choo, choo choo, riding on the train.
Now the train is speeding up! Chug chug chug chug chug chug! *(bounce child quickly)*
Choo choo, choo choo, riding on the train.
Choo choo, choo choo, riding on the train.
Now the train is slowing down. Chug chug chug chug chug chug! *(bounce child slowly)*
Choo choo, choo choo, riding on the train.
Choo choo, choo choo, riding on the train.
Wooo-wooo! The train stops!

> *Literacy bit:* "Books, rhymes, and songs about cars, trucks, planes, and trains allow you to imitate the sounds they make: 'beep beep,' 'zoom,' and 'chugga chugga.' Sounds like these help your child learn the sounds of language and will help your child develop pre-reading skills."

117 Trot, Trot (adapted traditional)

Trot, trot to Boston,
Trot, trot to Lynn.
Take care, baby.
Don't fall in.

Trot, trot to New York,
Trotting on past.
Hold tight, baby,
Let's trot fast!

Trot, trot to Washington,
A-trotting we will go.
Come on, baby,
Let's trot slow.

Trot, trot to *(your town),*
Home is in sight.
Hug those babies,
Squeeze them tight.

> *Literacy bit:* "When you adapt rhymes, songs, and stories to include people and places familiar to your child, you help him develop a greater understanding of his world."

118 Weather Bounce (to the tune of "London Bridge")

How the rain comes falling down, *(bounce child on lap)*
Falling down, falling down.
How the rain comes falling down,
On a rainy day.

Feel the way the wind does blow, *(sway child back and forth)*
Wind does blow, wind does blow.
Feel the way the wind does blow,
On a windy day.

We move slowly when it's hot, *(bounce child in slow motion)*
When it's hot, when it's hot.
We move slowly when it's hot,
On a hot, hot day.

Snuggle up when it is cold, *(snuggle child)*
It is cold, it is cold.
Snuggle up when it is cold,
On a cold, cold day.

> *Literacy bit:* "Rhymes about the natural world will help your child make language connections to the things she is experiencing each day."

119 The Wind

The wind blows me to the left, *(blow on child and move child left)*
The wind blows me to the right, *(blow on child and move child right)*
The wind blows me higher and higher out of sight! *(blow on child and lift him in the air)*

> *Literacy bit:* "Babies love to experience the natural world. Gently blowing on them during this rhyme will remind them of the wind."

• • •

Check out these entries in other chapters for more bouncing and movement:

The Babies on the Bus, p. 22

Baby Danced the Polka, p. 18

Itsy-Bitsy Babies, p. 30

Just Like This, p. 61

Let's Go, Baby-o!, p. 29

Take Me Out to the Park, p. 42

This Is the Way a Baby Rides, p. 25

Tip Tip Dig Dig, p. 20

What Do We Do with the Baby?, p. 29

6

Tickles, Claps, and Taps

• •

MANY TRADITIONAL NURSERY rhymes and children's songs feature tickling, clapping, and tapping—all ways to stimulate a baby's nervous system and sense of rhythm. Traditional rhymes about shoeing horses, for example, encourage tapping on the bottoms of babies' feet, which in turn stimulates the nerves and muscles there in preparation for the task of walking (Feierabend 2000). Clapping rhymes stimulate the palms, which will be used for many tasks as a child grows.

120 Baby Corn

I went to the picnic and what did I see?
A little ear of corn smiling at me!
I slathered it with butter *(rub hands over baby's belly)*
And rubbed my tum, *(rub tummy)*
Sprinkled salt and pepper on, *(mime sprinkling salt and pepper on baby)*
Then *yum, yum, yum! (pretend to eat baby's tummy)*

> *Literacy bit:* "Interacting and being silly with your child will help him feel safe and secure."

121 Beach Ball Balance (to the tune of "Surfin' U.S.A.")

Pass out beach balls and ask each caregiver to hold her child securely, belly down, on the ball while singing this song.

If every baby had a beach ball
Across the U.S.A.
Then every baby'd be balancin'
Like we are today.
You'd see 'em wearin' their diapers
And their onesies too.
Happy mommies and daddies
Balancin' today!

> *Literacy bit:* "Balancing on a beach ball or other large, round ball promotes a baby's sense of balance and upper body strength. These physical skills are important prerequisites to academic learning."

122 Birdie Tickle

Babies should be lying on their backs for this rhyme. Pass out pom-poms to caregivers and ask them to move the pom-poms in the air above the babies and tickle the babies' ears when the rhyme indicates.

Birdie flies across the sky,
Flying low and flying high,
Flying left and flying right,
Flying up and out of sight.
Come back, birdie, come back down!
Birdie circles to the ground.
Then when birdie's getting weary,
He lands gently on your ear-y!

> *Literacy bit:* "The visual tracking in this activity helps your baby practice using both eyes together, an important developmental skill for later reading. The soft pom-pom gives babies an experience of texture."

123 Birdie's Feather

Babies should be lying on their backs for this activity. Pass out feathers to caregivers and ask them to move the feathers in the air above the babies and tickle the body parts when the rhyme indicates.

Birdie flies away from her nest,
While her feather falls and tickles my chest.
Birdie lands in a nearby tree,
Her feather tickles both of my knees.
Birdie glides in the air nice and slow,
Then her feather tickles my toe.

Birdie and her friend play hide-and-seek,
While her feather tickles both of my cheeks!
Mother bird calls, "Come home, dear,"
And there's one last tickle on my ears.

> *Literacy bit:* "In this rhyme, your baby experiences the texture of a tickly feather. Touching a variety of textures is one way your baby explores the world."

124 Bumblebee Buzz

Babies should by lying on their backs for this activity. Pass out pom-poms to caregivers and ask them to move the pom-poms in the air above the babies as the rhyme indicates.

Bumblebee, bumblebee, buzzing around.
Up to the sky and down to the ground.
Buzz in a circle, in a wiggly line too,
Then he buzzes right down and tickles you!

> *Literacy bit:* "Making sounds is the first way your child tries to imitate speech and builds beginning language skills."

125 Clapping

Clapping little,
Clapping big,
Clap in a circle, rig-a-jig, jig.
Clap with a smile,
Clap with a frown,
Clapping up and clapping down.
Clap all night,
Clap all day,
Clap for my baby,
Hip-hip-hooray!

> *Literacy bit:* "Clapping rhymes like this one stimulate the nerves of the palms and help babies develop muscles that will later be used for writing."

126 Color, Color

Encourage caregivers to mime coloring on babies as you say this silly rhyme.

Color, color up and down,
Color, color all around.
Color, color knees and toes,
Color, color on your nose.
Color, color on your tummy,
Color, color on your mommy!

Literacy bit: "Repetition is key to the way that babies learn about the world. The repeated pattern in this rhyme gives a sense of security, building up suspense to the surprise at the end. Don't be surprised if your baby wants you to repeat it right away!"

127 Cuddles

Here is my nose,
Here is your nose,
Nuzzle nuzzle noses.
Here are my toes,
Here are your toes,
Nuzzle nuzzle toesies.
Here are your hands,
Here are my hands,
Give a little clap.
You can cuddle,
I can cuddle,
Curl up in my lap!

Literacy bit: "When babies feel loved and secure, they feel more confident to explore the world around them."

128 Ducky Tickle

Pass out rubber ducks or pom-poms and encourage caregivers to use them to act out the rhyme.

Quack, quack, quack,
The duck's on your back.
She climbs to your head,
And jumps to your lap.
Flap, flap, flap,
Down your legs she taps.
She waddles to your toes,
And back to your lap.
Skip, skip, skip,
Our ducky does flips.
She gives you a big kiss,
Right on your lips.

Literacy bit: "When you play with your baby, have fun making noises for the animals. Hearing different noises with various pitches, tones, and volumes helps your baby develop the basics of language."

129 Flying

Babies should be lying on their backs for this activity. Pass out scarves to caregivers and ask them to move the scarves in the air above the babies and tickle the body parts the rhyme indicates.

Flying through the air,
Oh what a sight.
The butterfly's wings have taken flight.
They fly up high,
They fly down low, *(tickle child's nose)*
They fly around and around
Before they go! *(tickle baby's tummy)*

> *Literacy bit:* "The visual tracking in this activity helps your baby practice using both eyes together, an important developmental skill for later reading."

130 Horsey Shoe

Encourage caregivers to tap the bottoms of babies' feet while saying the rhyme.

Horsey, horsey needs a shoe,
Horsey, horsey don't be blue.
Tap the bottom,
Tap the top.
Tap in a circle,
Don't you stop.
Horsey, horsey loves his shoe.
Horsey, horsey says thank you!

> *Literacy bit:* "Gently tapping the bottoms of babies' feet aids development toward walking."

131 Just Like This

Hug the baby, hug the baby,
Give a little clap.
Rock the baby, rock the baby,
Bounce her in your lap.
Tickle the baby, tickle the baby,
Give a little kiss.
Then lift the baby in the air
Just like this!

> *Literacy bit:* "Narrating actions through engaging rhymes like this one helps your baby develop vocabulary."

132 Kitty in the Tree

One little squirrel climbed up the tree, *(race fingers up child's body with lightest of pressure)*
Stopped at the top, what did she see?
Kitty followed squirrel up the tree, *(race fingers up child's body with slightly heavier pressure)*
Stopped at the top, what did she see?
It was such a long way down
That cat was scared and cried, "Meow!"
Here comes the fire truck through the town,
All to help get kitty down.
Firefighter climbs up in the tree, *(walk fingers up child's body more slowly, with heavier pressure)*
Brings down kitty, safe as can be! *(walk fingers back down to toes)*

> *Literacy bit:* "Tapping helps with proprioceptive development, which helps children understand where they are in space. Changing voices to match actions in the rhyme will help the child hear the sounds that make up speech."

133 Little Frog

Encourage caregivers to tap on babies' arms or legs, following the motions of the frog.

Ribbit, ribbit, said the frog.
There he sat upon the log.
He hopped to the left,
And he hopped to the right,
He leaped up high with all his might!
He hopped down the log with a great big dash,
And he hopped in the water with a great big splash!

> *Literacy bit:* "Gently tapping on your child during rhymes helps her sensory skills develop and allows her to sense the rhythm of language."

134 Little Mouse: A Rhyme from Lithuania (adapted traditional)

Little mouse *(wiggle finger)*
In her house
Stirred a porridge for her children. *(use index finger to "stir" on baby's palm)*
A pot for one, *(touch baby's index finger)*
A cup for another, *(touch baby's middle finger)*
A ladle for the third, *(touch baby's ring finger)*
A spoon for the fourth, *(touch baby's pinkie)*
And none for a little baby. *(clasp baby's thumb)*

Oh, dear,
Run, run, little mouse *(race fingers up baby's arm)*
To fetch some water. *(tickle baby's armpit)*

> *Literacy bit:* "Children internalize numbers by hearing counting again and again in nursery rhymes and songs. Counting helps your child develop mathematical and sequencing skills."

135 Milk the Cow (to the tune of "Row, Row, Row Your Boat")

Children can be lying on their backs for this song.

Milk, milk, milk the cow, *("milk" child's arms, legs, or hands with gentle strokes)*
Milking's what we do.
And when the milking is all done,
The cow says, "Mooooooo!" *(tickle child's stomach)*

> *Literacy bit:* "Light massage stimulates your baby's circulatory system and enhances bonding."

136 The Moon Is Round (traditional)

The moon is round, *(draw a semicircle on one side of the child's face)*
The moon is round. *(draw a semicircle on the other side of the child's face)*
It has two eyes, *(gently touch child's eyelids)*
A nose, *(gently touch child's nose)*
But knows no sound. *(press finger to child's lips)*

> *Literacy bit:* "The gentle repetition and soothing *o* sounds in this rhyme make it a perfect settling-down rhyme for bedtime or naptime."

137 One to Five

One little nose,
Two little feet,
Three little tickles on your tummy so sweet!
Four little kisses on five little toes,
Then one more kiss for your sweet little nose!

> *Literacy bit:* "Babies' strongest sense is the sense of touch. Using touch in simple rhymes like this one increases security and bonding."

138 **Pizza Baby**

Knead the dough,
Pizza baby, pizza baby, pizza baby. *(knead the baby's tummy)*
Spread the sauce,
Pizza baby, pizza baby, pizza baby. *(smooth hands on the baby's tummy)*
Sprinkle the cheese,
Pizza baby, pizza baby, pizza baby. *(tap on the baby's tummy)*
Eat it up,
Pizza baby, pizza baby, pizza baby. *(kiss the baby's tummy)*

> *Literacy bit:* "When babies experience different types of gentle touch and move-ment, their proprioceptive system is stimulated. This system is vital for let-ting your child know where he is in space and where he begins and others end. Children with well-developed proprioceptive systems are better able to focus and learn in the school years."

139 **Raindrops** (to the tune of "Twinkle Twinkle")

Encourage caregivers to gently tap the body parts described as you sing the song.

Raindrops falling all around,
Raindrops falling to the ground.
On your head, on your ear,
On your tummy, on your rear.
Raindrops falling on your toes.
Raindrops falling on your nose!

> *Literacy bit:* "Songs and rhymes about body parts allow children to begin to develop their sense of self and make associations between words and parts of the body."

140 **Rubba Dubba Ducky**

Pass out rubber duckies or yellow pom-poms and encourage caregivers to use them to tickle the babies during this rhyme.

Rubba dubba ducky, swimming in my bath,
We wash and we play and we splash splash splash.
My little rubber ducky is oh so funny,
We always laugh when I wash my tummy!

> *Literacy bit:* "Make up songs or rhymes about everyday activities with your child. As she gets older, encourage her to do the same. Singing and chanting rhymes are ways of practicing and exploring language."

141 **Snowflakes** (to the tune of "London Bridge")

Encourage caregivers to use their index fingers to show the snowflake falling through the air and landing on the baby's body in the place indicated in each verse.

Here's a snowflake falling down,
Falling down, falling down.
Here's a snowflake falling down,
On your arm.

> Repeat with *nose, toes, head, ear, tummy,* and other body parts as desired.

> *Literacy bit:* "Babies build visual tracking skills by following your finger through the air. This helps develop the eye muscles that will later be used to track text across a page. The suspense generated by changing the landing place of the snowflake in each verse keeps babies engaged."

142 **Teddy Bear**

Give teddy a hug, *(hug baby)*
Give teddy a squeeze, *(squeeze baby gently)*
Give teddy a tickle on his knees! *(tickle baby's knees)*
Give teddy a kiss, *(kiss baby)*
Give teddy a drum, *(drum fingers on baby's tummy)*
Give teddy a tickle on his tum! *(tickle baby's tummy)*

> *Literacy bit:* "Caregivers create a sense of security and love by interacting in fun and loving ways with the baby. Young children who feel safe and secure are better able to learn."

143 **There Was a Little Mouse: A Rhyme from Sweden** (adapted traditional)

There was a little mouse *(wiggle finger)*
Who wanted to come in the house. *(make finger run up baby's leg)*
Not here, not there, *(tickle various spots)*
But there! Squeak! *(tickle baby's most ticklish spot)*

> *Literacy bit:* "You are your child's first teacher. Fun and silly interactions like this may seem meaningless, but in fact your baby is absorbing vocabulary and the rhythm of speech each time you talk to him."

144 **Up, Up the Ladder** (traditional)

Up, up the ladder *(walk fingers up baby's arm)*
Hurry to the slide.
Sit at the top
Then down you slide! *(slide fingers down baby's arm)*

Literacy bit: "During this rhyme, your baby gets a multisensory experience of the concepts of up and down. Stimulating multiple senses aids the brain in understanding and retention."

145 Where Do They Go?

Where do your shoes go?
There, there, there. *(tap bottoms of baby's feet)*
Where does your hat go?
Hair, hair, hair. *(tap baby's head)*
Where does the food go?
In your tum. *(tap baby's tummy)*
Where does your diaper go?
On your bum! *(tap baby's bottom)*

> *Literacy bit:* "Rhymes about body parts allow children to begin to gain awareness of themselves as individuals separate from their caregivers."

146 Windy Day

Teach the sign WIND and encourage caregivers to gently blow on baby as indicated in the rhyme.

Out we went on a windy day, *(sign WIND)*
The wind said hello and wanted to play.
Wind on my forehead,
Wind on my nose,
Wind on my tummy,
Wind on my toes.
Wind blew hard and I said please, *(sign WIND forcefully)*
Wind blew gently, and it became a breeze. *(sign WIND gently)*

> *Literacy bit:* "Teaching basic American Sign Language to your baby helps her develop a deeper understanding of concepts. Many signs in ASL incorporate aspects of the concept they represent, and so can help children generate a mental picture of the concept. WIND is one of these, as it shows something moving in the wind. When you combine the sign with the sensory experience of blowing on your child, she can see and feel what the wind is like. Experiential learning such as this strengthens brain connections and deepens understanding and retention."

• • •

Check out these entries in other chapters for more tickling, clapping, and tapping:

7

Storytelling with Flannelboards, Magnetboards, and Props

••

IN STORYTIMES FOR other age groups, flannelboards and props are vital for adding interest and engaging participants. The same may be true for baby storytimes, but the ways we use those items must be adapted to encourage interaction between the caregiver and child. Flannelboard stories presented to the large group may still work, especially when presented as a storytelling model for the caregivers, but these flannelboard stories will work even better if the babies can interact with them in some way. For example, each child, with help, can put a shape on the board in the course of the story.

Other props can be equally effective, especially when they are small and inexpensive enough that each caregiver can take one. Pom-poms, for example, can be used with various rhymes about spiders and mice to create an experience of texture for the babies. When using other large props, such as puppets, be sure to take the time to bring the puppet to each child. (This is especially important because very young babies will not be able to see the puppet unless you do so!) In this chapter, we provide lots of specific suggestions for stories, songs, and rhymes using props, but we hope that you will also find these ideas a model for adapting other favorites for a baby storytime audience.

147 Around Town (to the tune of "Hi-Ho, the Derry-o")

Around town I must go,
Around town I must go,
Around town I must go-e-o,
Around town I must go.

(spoken) How will I get to town? *(place piece on board)* I'll drive the car! Here's how you sign CAR in American Sign Language.

We'll drive the car through town, *(sign CAR)*
We'll drive the car through town,
We'll drive the car through town-e-o,
We'll drive the car through town.

Repeat with other means of transportation.

Literacy bit: "Babies love to talk about cars, planes, trains, and other types of transportation! When you teach your child the signs for these items, he can tell you about them even before he learns to speak. This allows your child to start a conversation on a topic he is interested in, and then when you talk back, he's already engaged and ready to take in all of that spoken vocabulary you are giving him, which leads to development of spoken language. In this way, signing with babies actually enhances spoken language development."

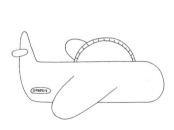

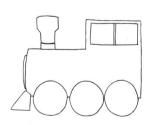

148 **Baby's Lunch**

It was lunchtime, and the baby was *sooooo* hungry.

Mommy and Daddy went to visit the cow. "Please, Ms. Cow," they said, "will you give us some milk for our hungry baby?"

And the cow said yes! So Mommy and Daddy gave Baby some milk, but . . . Baby was *still* hungry!

So Mommy and Daddy went to visit the chicken. "Please, Ms. Chicken," they said, "will you give us some eggs for our hungry baby?"

And the chicken said yes! So Mommy and Daddy scrambled up the eggs and gave them to Baby, but . . . Baby was *still* hungry!

So Mommy and Daddy went to visit the apple tree. "Please, Apple Tree," they said, "will you give us some apples for our hungry baby?"

And the tree said yes! So Mommy and Daddy gathered up some apples and took them home and made some yummy applesauce for Baby. Baby ate it all up, but . . . Baby was *still* hungry!

So Mommy and Daddy went to visit the baker. "Please, Mr. Baker," they said, "will you give us some bread for our hungry baby?"

And the baker said yes! So Mommy and Daddy gave Baby some yummy bread, and . . . finally Baby was full!

"Thank you!" said Baby, and then she curled up and went to sleep.

Literacy bit: "You can tell simple stories like this one using everyday objects in your home. By telling stories with objects from her daily life, you help your baby associate the items with the words she hears."

149 Blocks

Use soft blocks and a toy car to act out this rhyme.

I stack my blocks, one, two, three,
And down they fall right next to me.
I stack my blocks, one, two, three, four,
This time I could stack even more.
I add another block, one, two, three, four, five,
Then put my toy car into drive!
Crash!

> *Literacy bit:* "Putting parts together will help your child learn to solve problems. Build towers of blocks and crash them to demonstrate cause and effect."

150 Boo-Boo Bear

Use a stuffed bear and bandages to help you tell this story.

This is my friend Bear. He's not always as careful as he should be, and sometimes he has an accident. Sometimes he gets hurt. Here's how we say HURT in American Sign Language. Bear can tell me where it hurts when he uses that sign at the place where it hurts. One day, Bear fell down and scraped his knee, so he signed it here *(sign HURT at bear's knee)*. There, there, Bear, we'll clean it up and put on a bandage. And a kiss to make it feel better.

Later that day, a bee stung Bear right on his ear! Bear told me about it by signing HURT right by his ear. There, there, Bear, we'll clean it up and put on a bandage. And a kiss to make it feel better.

The next day, Bear opened a card from his aunt and got a paper cut on his finger. Bear told me about it by signing HURT and pointing to his finger. There, there, Bear, we'll clean it up and put on a bandage. And a kiss to make it feel better.

And then Bear opened the door too quickly and scraped his nose! Bear told me about it by signing HURT right by his nose. There, there, Bear, we'll clean it up and put on a bandage. And a kiss to make it feel better.

Then Bear went to the beach and stepped on a sharp seashell! Bear told me about it by signing HURT right by his foot. There, there, Bear, we'll clean it up and put on a bandage. And a kiss to make it feel better.

Let's count the bandages!

If desired, let each child help you put on a bandage and then count them all.

> *Literacy bit:* "Teaching your child simple signs like HURT allows him to tell you what he is thinking and feeling before he can speak and can significantly reduce frustration for both of you! Even after your child begins to speak, supporting speech with simple signs can reduce frustration about words that are difficult for young children to pronounce."

151 **Bubbles in My Bath** (to the tune of "Ten Green Bottles")

One little bubble floating in my bath,
One little bubble floating in my bath,
And if one more bubble should come to play like that,
There'll be two little bubbles floating in my bath.

Two little bubbles . . .
Three little bubbles . . .
Four little bubbles . . .
Five little bubbles . . .
And then . . . the bubbles *pop! (clap five times, removing a bubble each time)*
No more bubbles!

> *Literacy bit:* "Counting books and rhymes help children learn sequencing skills that develop narrative skills. Children who can tell sequenced rhymes and stories can more easily tell narrative stories."

152 **Counting Cookies**

Stick magnet-backed cookie shapes onto a metal baking pan and hold it up to show everyone.

Counting cookies on the tray,
Counting cookies on the tray,
Counting cookies on the tray,
How many cookies do I see today?
One, two, three!

Repeat, varying the number of cookies on the tray each time.

> *Literacy bit:* "Counting in rhymes and songs helps your child develop mathematical and sequencing skills."

153 **Feel-Better Soup** (loosely based on the book *Monkey Soup* by Louis Sachar. New York: Knopf, 1992)

Tell this as a prop story or use flannelboard or magnetboard pieces. You will need the following props:

- a laundry basket
- a stuffed animal
- bubbles
- paper

- tissues
- crayons
- a toy
- a storybook
- a wooden spoon

If you choose to tell this story with a magnetboard or flannelboard, consider using a real laundry basket and wooden spoon to stir the pieces.

Baby doesn't feel good—she's sick, sick, sick! She has a runny nose and her tummy feels funny. Daddy bundled her up and gave her some medicine, but she still felt cranky. So Daddy said, "You need some special Feel-Better Soup!"

He got a big basket. "First, we need a special friend to cuddle with." He put the stuffed animal into the soup.

"Next we need some tissues for that runny nose." And he put the tissues into the soup.

"Ah-choo!" said Baby, and everything in the soup went flying.

"Oh, dear," said Daddy, and he picked up the stuffed animal and the tissues and put them back in the soup. He gave it a stir and said, "What else do we need in our Feel-Better Soup? How about some crayons and paper for drawing? That will help you feel better." He put the crayons and paper into the soup.

"Next we need some bubbles to blow." And he blew some bubbles and put the bottle into the soup.

"Aaaaaah-choo!" said Baby, and everything in the soup went flying *again*.

"Oh, dear," said Daddy, and he picked up the ingredients and put them back in the soup. He gave it a stir and said, "It's not quite done yet. What else do we need in our Feel-Better Soup?"

Baby thought and thought, but she didn't know.

"I've got it!" said Daddy. "How about a toy horse to play with? That always makes me feel better." And he put the toy horse into the soup.

Baby was feeling better already. That horse looked like fun.

"And one more special ingredient," said Daddy. "A storybook." He put the book into the soup.

Baby reached for the spoon.

"Would you like to stir the soup?" asked Daddy. "Here you go."

And Baby stirred and stirred the soup until . . . "Aaaaaaaaaaah-*choo!*" said Baby, and everything went flying. But by then Baby was feeling better, so they played with all the toys.

"What do you know?" said Daddy. "Feel-Better Soup really works!"

> *Literacy bit:* "Telling simple stories during everyday events or difficult times helps young children make sense of their experiences."

154 Five Hopping Frogs

One frog hopping alone in the morning dew,
He heard another—*ribbit!*—and then there were two.
Two frogs hopping beneath a willow tree,
They heard another—*ribbit!*—and then there were three.
Three frogs hopping past the alligator as he let out a snore,
They heard another—*ribbit!*—and then there were four.
Four frogs hopping near the pond take a dive,
They heard another—*ribbit!*—and then there were five.

> *Literacy bit:* "Though rhymes like this one may seem simple, they actually teach many concepts in an engaging way. Babies internalize counting concepts when they hear them over and over in rhymes. The rhythm and rhyme help babies develop phonological awareness, or a sense of the smaller parts of words. The content of the rhyme teaches about the natural world as it discusses the kinds of things that frogs do."

155 Five Silly Clowns (to the tune of "Five Little Ducks")

One silly clown went out to play
In the circus tent one day.
He had such enormous fun,
He called for another little clown to come.

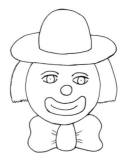

Two silly clowns . . .
Three silly clowns . . .
Four silly clowns . . .

Five silly clowns went out to play
In the circus tent one day.
They had such enormous fun,
And all tumbled home when the circus was done.

> *Literacy bit:* "Babies and young children learn through repetition! Each time they hear a rhyme, song, or story, they pick up something new about it."

156 I Have a Pet

Present this game with flannelboard pieces or puppets. Hide the animal until you have revealed its identity, and then repeat the information about it so the babies can make language connections.

I have a pet, he's soft and brown. When he's happy he wags his tail and says, "Woof-woof."

What is he?

It's a doggie! Look how soft his fur is. He says, "Woof-woof," as he wags his tail.

I have a pet with beautiful feathers. When she's happy, she sings, "Tweet-tweet."

What is she?

It's a bird! Look at her beautiful feathers. "Tweet-tweet," says the birdie!

I have a pet with pointy ears and a long tail. When she's happy, she purrs and says, "Me-ow."

What is she?

It's a kitty-cat! The kitty has soft fur and a long tail. Sometimes she says, "Me-ow," and sometimes, when she is very happy, she purrs!

I have a pet that swims through the water. When I feed him, he races to the top of the water and says, "Glub-glub."

What is he?

It's a fish! He loves to swim, and he goes like this when he eats his food *(make fish face)*. "Glub-glub," says the fishy!

I have a pet, an unusual pet. He coils himself around my arm and says, "Hiss-hiss."

What is he?

It's a snake! His scales feel smooth. He likes to coil himself up and say, "Hiss-hiss."

> *Literacy bit:* "Playing guessing games helps your child learn listening skills. You can play these games with your child even before she can speak. Just pause for a few moments after you ask the question, and then supply the answer yourself. In the very youngest babies, this models turn-taking in conversation. As your child gets older, however, make sure that you pause long enough to allow your child to answer. Adults tend to give children no more than *one second* to respond before the adult repeats or rephrases. Giving your child the gift of your patient attention helps her develop confidence and sends the message that you care to hear what she has to say!"

157 Ice Cream

I went to the ice cream shop,
There were so many flavors I couldn't stop!
First I picked my favorite cone,
And added a scoop of chocolate so it wasn't alone.
Mom asked if I wanted more,
So I decided to add all the flavors in the store!

Add scoops of ice cream and say the color with the flavor, then count the scoops.

My ice cream cone was so tall and high,
That suddenly it began to fall . . . sigh!

> *Literacy bit:* "Knowing colors is an important skill that all children need to learn. Like knowing numbers and the names of the letters of the alphabet, this skill is best learned through repetition in the context of everyday events. Talk about colors when you use crayons or other items. Color identification games are a great way to while away waiting-room time, too!"

158 Into the Bathtub

Present this rhyme as a flannelboard, or make a "bathtub" from a box and act out the rhyme with props.

Into the bathtub my ducky must go,
Or I refuse to put in even my toe.
Into the bathtub my bubbles must go,
Or I refuse to put in even my toe.
Into the bathtub my fish must go,
Or I refuse to put in even my toe.
Into the bathtub my fishing rod must go,
Or I refuse to put in even my toe.
Into the bathtub my pirate ship must go,
Or I refuse to put in even my toe.
Into the bathtub I must go,
Oh no, I can't even fit my toe!

> *Literacy bit:* "Stories, rhymes, and songs about everyday routines will help your child develop narrative skills."

159 It's Baby's Birthday

Tell this story using a flannelboard or magnetboard, or as a prop story using a doll or stuffed animal, a crown, a balloon, a garland, a box with a teddy bear inside, and a toy birthday cake.

It's Baby's birthday!

He wears a special crown to show what a special day this is.

Mommy and Daddy have decorated the house with balloons and streamers.

Look, Grandma has brought Baby a present. What could be inside?

Baby opens up the box. It's a teddy!

Thank you, Grandma!

Mommy says it's time to bring in the cake. She turns off the light, and for a moment Baby is scared. But then he sees Mommy coming with a special birthday cake. And it has pretty candles on it!

Everyone sings: "Happy birthday to you, happy birthday to you, happy birthday, dear Baby, happy birthday to you!"

"Blow out the candles, Baby!" And Baby blows and blows until the candles all go out.

"Hooray!" shouts everyone. "Happy Birthday, Baby!"

> *Literacy bit:* "Listening to stories about special events helps babies know what to expect and develop a greater sense of security."

160 *Just Ducky* **by Kathy Mallat. New York: Walker, 2002.**

A little duckling can't find anyone to play with him, until he makes friends with his reflection in the water.

Try telling this story with puppets!

You will need

- two identical duckling puppets
- a bee puppet
- a mouse puppet
- a frog puppet
- a clear glass- or plastic-topped table

Use the puppets to act out the story. When the duckling sees his reflection in the water, place one duckling above the table and the other below. Move them in mirror images of one another as the duckling floats, splashes, and rolls. Also consider spritzing the children with water from a spray bottle when the duckling splashes!

Literacy bit: "Babies learn about basic scientific concepts such as cause and effect, gravity, and reflection through experience and through stories."

161 **Little Miss Muffet**

Tie a string around the middle of a large black pom-pom. Cut six 1-inch lengths of black pipe cleaner and bend each into an S-shape. Hot glue the pipe cleaners to the sides of the pom-pom to make the legs. Add googly eyes to complete the spider. Tie the other end of the string to a stick. Sit a doll in a chair and slowly lower the spider over her as you say the rhyme, and then make her run away. Repeat the rhyme using the children's names, and take the spider to visit each child.

Little Miss Muffet
Sat on a tuffet,
Eating her curds and whey.
Along came a spider
And sat down beside her
And frightened Miss Muffet away!

Literacy bit: "Children internalize the rhythms of language through repetition of nursery rhymes and songs. When you adapt traditional rhymes to include your child's name, you create a greater sense of engagement with language."

162 Polly, Put the Kettle On (traditional)

Present this rhyme as a magnetboard, flannelboard, or prop rhyme. To present it as a prop rhyme, use a toy teakettle and a paper plate with a spiral drawn on it for a burner.

Polly, put the kettle on,
Polly, put the kettle on,
Polly, put the kettle on,
We'll all have tea.

Sukey, take it off again,
Sukey, take it off again,
Sukey, take it off again,
They've all gone away.

Repeat using babies' names, and give each child a chance to put the kettle on or take it off the burner.

Literacy bit: "This rhyme emphasizes opposites through words and actions, giving babies a more solid understanding of 'on' and 'off.'"

 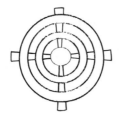

163 Pumpkin Faces (to the tune of "Frère Jacques")

Print two large pumpkins from the patterns on the website and laminate them. When you present the song, use a dry-erase marker to draw on the appropriate face. Describe the face as you draw it. For example, you might say, "This pumpkin is smiling. See how the corners of his mouth turn up? That's how we know he is happy!"

Happy pumpkin, happy pumpkin,
See him smile, see him smile,
Sitting in the window,
Sitting in the window,
Happy smile,
Happy smile.

Sad pumpkin, sad pumpkin,
See him frown, see him frown,
Sitting in the window,
Sitting in the window,
Sad frown,
Sad frown.

Literacy bit: "Helping your child to put words to feelings develops vocabulary in a meaningful way. You can talk not only about your child's feelings but about yours as well. Children can understand the words long before they can say them."

164 Rabbits (to the tune of "Ten Green Bottles")

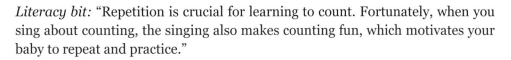

One little rabbit sitting in the sun.
One little rabbit sitting in the sun.
If one more rabbit should come and join the fun,
There'll be two little rabbits sitting in the sun.

Two little rabbits . . .
Three little rabbits . . .
Four little rabbits . . .

Five little rabbits sitting in the sun.
Five little rabbits sitting in the sun.
And if all five rabbits hop home when day is done,
There'll be no little rabbits sitting in the sun.

> *Literacy bit:* "Repetition is crucial for learning to count. Fortunately, when you sing about counting, the singing also makes counting fun, which motivates your baby to repeat and practice."

165 Shoe Game

Pass out two shoe pieces to each caregiver and encourage caregivers to place the pieces on their babies as you say the rhyme.

Here's a shoe, and here's a shoe,
Let's count them, one, two.
Where do the shoes go?
On your head, like so?
No, that's silly! How about here:
One shoe hanging from each ear?
That's not right! But now I've got 'em—
They go here, on your bottom!
No, they don't, that's just funny!
But I bet they go here on your tummy.
No? They don't? Well, isn't that sweet.
Look, they fit here on your feet!

> *Literacy bit:* "When adults act silly as in this rhyme, it not only amuses babies, but it also gives them a chance to show what they know as they begin to correct you! This helps babies develop confidence and expressive skills."

166 Springtime Ducklings (to the tune of "Five Little Ducks")

Five little ducklings went out one day,
Exploring the flowers and lost their way.
The mother duck said, "Quack, quack, quack,"
But only four little ducks came back.

Four little ducklings went out one day . . .
Three little ducklings went out one day . . .
Two little ducklings went out one day . . .
One little duckling went out one day . . .

"Wah, wah, wah," cried Mommy Duck.
She looked for her ducklings with no luck.
The mother duck said, "Quack, quack, quack."
And covered in flowers her ducklings came back!

> *Literacy bit:* "When you play with your baby, have fun making noises for the animals. Learning different noises with various pitches, tones, and volumes helps your baby develop the basics of language."

167 There Was an Old Woman Who Lived in a Shoe (adapted traditional)

Say the rhyme once, and then pass out simple figures cut from various colors of felt. Invite the babies and caregivers to come up and put their "children" on the flannelboard when you call their color.

There was an old woman who lived in a shoe.
She had so many children, but she knew what to do.
She gave them some milk, and she gave them some bread,
And she gave them all kisses, and tucked them in bed.

There was an old woman who lived in a shoe.
She had so many *red* children . . .

> Repeat with other colors.

> *Literacy bit:* "Repetition is crucial to the way young children learn. Your baby will want to hear the same rhymes and songs and stories over and over again, because each time he is internalizing something new from them."

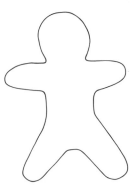

168 **Three Jellyfish** (traditional)

Present this traditional song with a flannelboard or magnetboard, American Sign Language, or both. See a video demonstrating the song with signs at www.storytimestuff.net.

THREE JELLYFISH,
THREE JELLYFISH,
THREE JELLYFISH SITTING on a ROCK.
Zoop! ONE JUMPED off!

TWO JELLYFISH . . .
ONE JELLYFISH . . .
NO JELLYFISH . . .

But then . . . *zoop!* ONE JELLYFISH JUMPED back on.
Zoop! Another JELLYFISH JUMPED back on.
Zoop! Another JELLYFISH JUMPED back on.
Let's count them! ONE . . . TWO . . . THREE!

THREE JELLYFISH,
THREE JELLYFISH,
THREE JELLYFISH SITTING on a ROCK.

> *Literacy bit:* "Using basic signs with songs helps your child not only develop manual dexterity, which will later be important for grasping and holding things and for writing, but also make connections with concepts and language. This song uses a simple story to emphasize opposites."

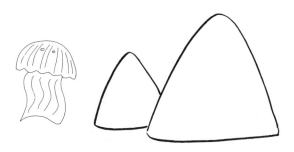

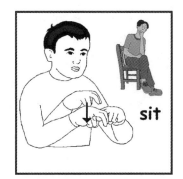

rock

jump

two

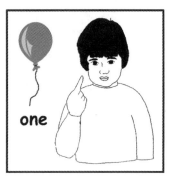

one

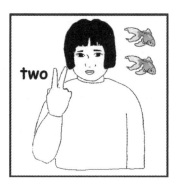

169 Time for Bed

"It's time for bed," my mama said.
"I won't go down," I said with a frown.
"What if you have your special blankie?" Mama asked while waving a hankie.
"I won't go down," I said with a frown.
"What if you have your special book?" said Mama as she took the book from its nook.
"I won't go down," I said with a frown.
"What if you have your special song?" Mama asked and sang along.
"I won't go down," I said with a frown.
"What if we turn your lights down low?" said Mama in the light's soft glow.
"I won't *(yawn)* go down," I said with a frown.
"What if we tuck in teddy, too?" said Mama as she tucked my bear named Lou.
I slid right down. "Zzzzzz." Safe and sound.

Literacy bit: "Rhyming chunks of words helps your child learn the smaller sounds of language."

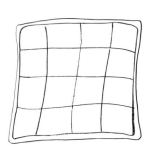

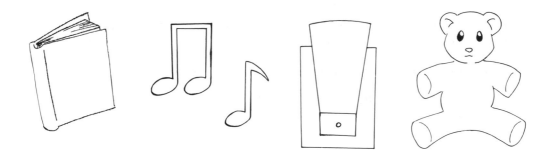

170 Under the Nighttime Sky

Present this rhyme using a flannelboard, a magnetboard, or stick puppets of the pieces.

Under the sky, the nighttime sky,
We look up at the moon.
The moon's bright light shines through the night
As we sing a little tune, la-la-la.
The owl says, "Who? Who are you?"
And we tell him who we are.
Then something bright moves through the night—
We found a shooting star!

> *Literacy bit:* "Spending time outside exploring nature with your child will give you lots of opportunities to talk about new things that you see and do. Having a wide range of experiences will give your child a good foundation for reading comprehension."

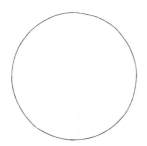

171 What Bear Likes Best

Use a stuffed bear with the flannelboard pieces to tell the story. If you don't have a bear, substitute a doll, a puppet, or another stuffed animal.

Bear likes fruit, but apples are his favorite. Which one do you like best?

When Bear wants a drink, he likes milk. What's your favorite? Do you prefer orange juice or water?

Bear likes to drink out of his sippy cup. What do you like to drink out of?

When Bear is ready to play, he looks for his ball. Do you like the ball or the swing best?

It's dress-up time! Which hat will Bear wear? He likes the firefighter hat! Which one is your favorite?

> *Literacy bit:* "When reading or telling stories, stop and ask your child questions throughout. This will engage her, even before she can respond, and help her internalize the concept of turn-taking in conversation."

172 **Where Is Baby's Pumpkin?**

Place the family members and the pumpkin behind the other pieces on the flannelboard or magnetboard as listed in the story, so that you can reveal them when the baby finds them.

It's autumn, and Baby is looking for his special pumpkin. Where could it be hiding?

Is Baby's pumpkin behind the tree?

No, that's a silly squirrel looking for acorns. Hello, squirrel!

Is Baby's pumpkin behind the car?

No, that's Mommy! Hello, Mommy!

Is Baby's pumpkin behind the swing set?

No, that's Daddy. Hello, Daddy!

Is Baby's pumpkin behind the cozy jacket?

No, that's Sister. Hello, Sister!

Is Baby's pumpkin under the pile of leaves?

No, that's Brother. Hello, Brother!

Is Baby's pumpkin behind the house?

Yes, there is Baby's pumpkin.

Come on, Mommy, Daddy, Sister, and Brother. Let's put a funny face on the pumpkin. Happy autumn!

> *Literacy bit:* "Repetition in stories helps your child develop prediction skills and confidence in language. This will help him develop the narrative skills to tell stories later on."

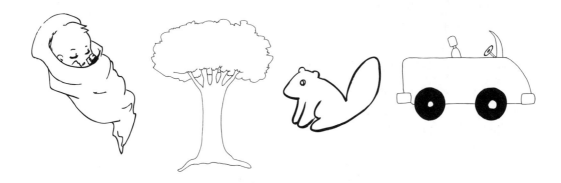

173 A Zoo on Our Heads

Use the tune of "Pig on Her Head" by Laurie Berkner on the CD *Buzz Buzz* (New York: Two Tomatoes, 1998) to share a silly song with the children. Pass out animal puppets or die-cut shapes of animals, and invite the caregivers to place them on the babies' heads as you sing the song. This song can be used for farm, zoo, jungle, or pet storytimes—simply adapt the animals you use to your theme. Then sing a verse using each child's name.

Katie has a sheep on her head,
Katie has a sheep on her head,
Katie has a sheep on her head,
She keeps it there all day.

> *Literacy bit:* "Children learn best through play. It helps them absorb new information without stress while engaging multiple senses. Don't be afraid to get silly!"

• • •

Check out these entries in other chapters for more fun with props, flannelboards, and magnetboards:

APPENDIX

Further Resources for Baby Storytime Planning

Acredolo, Linda P., and Susan Goodwyn. 2000. *Baby Minds: Brain-Building Games Your Baby Will Love*. New York: Bantam Books.

American Sign Language Clip and Create 5. 2005. Institute for Disabilities Research and Training, www.idrt.com.

Bahan, Ben, and Joe Dannis. 1990. *Signs for Me: Basic Sign Vocabulary for Children, Parents, and Teachers*. San Diego, CA: DawnSignPress.

Benjamin, Floella. 1995. *Skip Across the Ocean: Nursery Rhymes from around the World*. New York: Orchard Books.

Blakemore, Caroline, and Barbara Weston Ramirez. 2006. *Baby Read-Aloud Basics*. New York: AMACOM.

Blythe, Sally Goddard. 2006. *The Well-Balanced Child: Movement and Early Learning*. Gloucestershire, UK: Hawthorn Press.

Briant, Monta Z. 2006. *Sign, Sing, and Play! Fun Signing Activities for You and Your Baby*. Carlsbad, CA: Hay House.

Briant, Monta Z., and Susan Z. 2008. *Songs for Little Hands Activity Guide and CD*. Carlsbad, CA: Hay House.

Butler, Dorothy. 1998. *Babies Need Books*. Portsmouth, NH: Heinemann.

Carlson, Ann D. 2005. *Flannelboard Stories for Infants and Toddlers*. Chicago: American Library Association.

Cobb, Jane. 2007. *What'll I Do with the Baby-O? Nursery Rhymes, Songs, and Stories for Babies*. Vancouver, BC: Black Sheep Press. Book with CD.

Dennis, Kirsten, and Tressa Azpiri. 2005. *Sign to Learn: American Sign Language in the Early Childhood Classroom*. St. Paul, MN: Redleaf Press.

Ernst, Linda L. 2008. *Baby Rhyming Time*. New York: Neal-Schuman.

———. 1995. *Lapsit Services for the Very Young*. New York: Neal-Schuman.

———. 2005. *Lapsit Services for the Very Young II*. New York: Neal-Schuman.

Feierabend, John M. 2000. *The Book of Bounces*. Chicago: GIA Publications.

———. 2000. *The Book of Tapping and Clapping*. Chicago: GIA Publications.

Feierabend, John M., and Luann Saunders. 2000. *Frog in the Meadow: Music, Now I'm Two!* Chicago: GIA Publications.

Ghoting, Saroj Nadkarni, and Pamela Martin-Diaz. 2006. *Early Literacy Storytimes @ your library*. Chicago: American Library Association.

——. 2013. *Storytimes for Everyone! Developing Young Children's Language and Literacy*. Chicago: American Library Association.

Isbell, Christy. 2010. *Everyday Play: Fun Games to Develop the Fine Motor Skills Your Child Needs for School*. Silver Spring, MD: Gryphon House.

Jeffery, Debby Ann. 1995. *Literate Beginnings: Programs for Babies and Toddlers*. Chicago: American Library Association.

MacMillan, Kathy. 2008. *A Box Full of Tales: Easy Ways to Share Library Resources through Story Boxes*. Chicago: ALA Editions.

——. 2013. *Little Hands and Big Hands: Children and Adults Signing Together*. Chicago: Huron Street Press.

——. 2006. *Try Your Hand at This! Easy Ways to Incorporate Sign Language into Your Programs*. Lanham, MD: Scarecrow Press.

MacMillan, Kathy, and Christine Kirker. 2011. *Kindergarten Magic*. Chicago: ALA Editions.

——. 2012. *Multicultural Storytime Magic*. Chicago: ALA Editions.

——. 2009. *Storytime Magic: 400 Fingerplays, Flannelboards, and Other Activities*. Chicago: ALA Editions.

Marino, Jane, and Dorothy F. Houlihan. 2003. *Babies in the Library!* Lanham, MD: Scarecrow Press.

——. 1992. *Mother Goose Time: Library Programs for Babies and Their Caregivers*. New York: H. W. Wilson.

Mayes, Linda C., and Donald J. Cohen. 2002. *The Yale Child Study Center Guide to Understanding Your Child: Healthy Development from Birth to Adolescence*. Boston: Little, Brown.

Miller, Anne Meeker. 2008. *Mealtime and Bedtime Sing and Sign*. Philadelphia, PA: Da Capo Press.

——. 2007. *Toddler Sing and Sign*. New York: Marlowe.

Murray, Carol Garboden. 2007. *Simple Signing with Young Children: A Guide for Infant, Toddler, and Preschool Teachers*. Beltsville, MD: Gryphon House.

Nespeca, Sue McLeaf. 1994. *Library Programming for Families with Young Children*. New York: Neal-Schuman.

Odean, Kathleen. 2003. *Great Books for Babies and Toddlers*. New York: Ballantine.

Opie, Iona, ed. 1996. *My Very First Mother Goose*. Cambridge, MA: Candlewick.

Parlakian, Rebecca. 2003. *Before the ABCs: Promoting School Readiness in Infants and Toddlers*. Washington, DC: Zero to Three.

Raines, Shirley, Karen Miller, and Leah Curry-Rood. 2002. *Story S-t-r-e-t-c-h-e-r-s for Infants, Toddlers, and Twos: Experiences, Activities, and Games for Popular Children's Books*. Beltsville, MD: Gryphon House.

Rawson, Martyn, and Michael Rose. 2006. *Ready to Learn: From Birth to School Readiness*. Gloucestershire, UK: Hawthorn Press.

Sasse, Margaret. 2009. *Active Baby, Healthy Brain*. New York: The Experiment.

Schiller, Pam. 2005. *The Complete Resource Book for Infants*. Beltsville, MD: Gryphon House.

Schiller, Pam, and Jackie Silberg. 2003. *The Complete Book of Activities, Games, Stories, Props, Recipes, and Dances for Young Children*. Beltsville, MD: Gryphon House.

Shickedanz, Judith. 1999. *Much More Than the ABCs: The Early Stages of Reading and Writing*. Washington, DC: National Association for the Education of Young Children.

Shonkoff, Jack P., and Deborah A. Phillips, eds. 2000. *From Neurons to Neighborhoods: The Science of Early Childhood Development*. Washington, DC: National Academy Press.

Silberg, Jackie. 2012. *125 Brain Games for Babies: Simple Games to Promote Early Brain Development*. Lewisville, NC: Gryphon House.

Trevino, Rose Zertuche. 2009. *Read Me a Rhyme in Spanish and English*. Chicago: ALA Editions.

Warner, Penny. 2010. *Baby's Favorite Rhymes to Sign*. New York: Three Rivers Press.

Websites

Denver (Colorado) Public Library, "Babble, Scribble, Read!": http://kids.denverlibrary.org/grownups/early_literacy/1styear.html

Saroj Ghoting: www.earlylit.net

Signing Savvy: www.signingsavvy.com

Storytime Stuff: www.storytimestuff.net

Works Cited

Ernst, Linda L. 2008. *Baby Rhyming Time*. New York: Neal-Schuman.

Feierabend, John M. 2000. *The Book of Tapping and Clapping*. Chicago: GIA Publications.

Ghoting, Saroj Nadkarni, and Pamela Martin-Diaz. 2005. *Early Literacy Storytimes @ your library*. Chicago: American Library Association.

Johnson, Susan R. 2007. *You and Your Child's Health: Teaching Our Children to Write, Read, and Spell*. www.youandyourchildshealth.org

Maddigan, Beth, and Stefanie Drennan. 2003. *The Big Book of Stories , Songs, and Sing-Alongs: Programs for Babies, Toddlers, and Families*. Westport, CT: Libraries Unlimited.

Marino, Jane, and Dorothy F. Houlihan. 1992. *Mother Goose Time: Library Programs for Babies and Their Caregivers*. New York: H. W. Wilson.

Mayes, Linda C., and Donald J. Cohen. 2002. *The Yale Child Study Center Guide to Understanding Your Child: Healthy Development from Birth to Adolescence*. Boston: Little, Brown.

Nespeca, Sue McLeaf. 1994. *Library Programming for Families with Young Children*. New York: Neal-Schuman.

Odean, Kathleen. 2003. *Great Books for Babies and Toddlers*. New York: Ballantine.

Shelov, Steven, and Tanya Remer Altmann, eds. 2009. *Caring for Your Baby and Young Child: Birth to Age 5*. Elk Grove Village, IL: American Academy of Pediatrics.

Shonkoff, Jack P., and Deborah A. Phillips, eds. 2000. *From Neurons to Neighborhoods: The Science of Early Childhood Development*. Washington, DC: National Academy Press.

Index of Activities by Subject

General Index